MW01129112

CONTENTS

FOREWORD
Marty Roe - LHS Class of '79

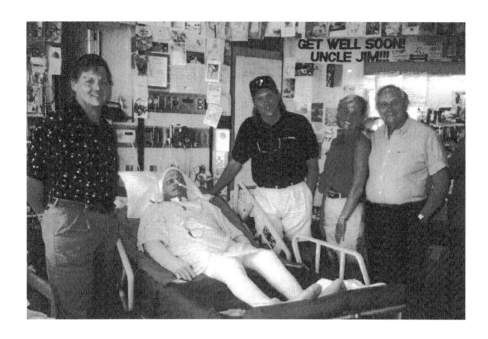

Writing a book is not all that different from writing a song. Usually, you have a specific idea or story you want to communicate to whomever your audience might turn out to be, it can take a long time or happen quite quickly. It is more about the journey, and this journey took much longer than any of us involved ever thought.

We began with a search for a ghostwriter, a person who might take on the project and budget issues. It looked as if it would die before we even got started, then Ty, brought up an old name from both of our pasts that was actually a very accomplished writer and very familiar with coach Jim VanDeGrift and his story, even from before either of us.

Joe Henderson was a sports writer and long-time writer for The Tampa Tribune. He grew up in Lebanon and got his start covering sports at the local newspaper, The Western Star.

Joe was my first football coach with the Lebanon PeeWee Elks and coached Ty and me. Ty called him, and Joe was immediately on board.

Joe has done a great job of capturing several of the many life-altering stories that took place in our little hometown. Thanks, in no small part to the witness of one man, Jim VanDeGrift.

Thank you, Joe, for your patience and talent.

When I first began talking to Ty VanDeGrift about getting his father to tell his story and the stories of all the lives that had come under his tutor ledge. We knew it would be difficult to get him to talk about the impact he has had on so many lives. Ty said if anyone could get him to allow us to pursue the idea of writing this book about his experience, it would be me. Thanks a lot, Ty.

Be that as it may, I called Jim and let him in on the concept. I told him that his story was one of great inspiration to me and many others and that it might be worthy of explaining it to a broader audience than just the ones directly influenced in Lebanon Ohio, where he has spent the majority of his life.

As expected, he was quite resistant to the idea at first. We talked at length about his desire to not "make this all about him." I assured him that this was a "God story," and he just happened to be the vessel in this instance.

We agreed that if not for the Love of Christ in his life, the results of his life and how it affected all those around him, would have been very different. My coach, Jim VanDeGrift, had experienced the miracle of Christ in his life and merely shared this love, through triumph and trial, in his own (to use his word) "hayseed" way.

I grew up in an "Ozzie and Harriet" family. My parents are two of the most wonderful people. They loved God and made sure I knew right from wrong. Although my Father was not much of a sports guy, he knew I loved sports. He and my mom were always there for me and never missed a game. As teens usually do, sometimes making the right choice while at school it was not as easy when your parents weren't looking.

But at school, I was blessed to have Coach in my life to reinforce the ethics and morals I was learning at home, and for a young man away from his parents, this was highly important.

Jim VanDeGrift, though he was not a perfect man (like I thought my father was) taught me how to be present and to be tough even while facing adversity. This incredible man took time to know who I was and wasn't afraid to "bust me" when I needed it and then be there to help me pick up the pieces when I felt like there was no way out.

Fast forward to 1993, I am now Marty Roe, the lead singer of an up and coming country band called Diamond Rio and was on tour with country legends "Alabama."

I got a call from my mom saying Coach is coming to your show and wants tickets and backstage passes, what do you say except "of course." That night after our set it was great to see him and so many of my old school mates for the first time in 14 years. Coach immediately greeted me with a big hug and looked at me with his piercing ice blue eyes and told me how proud he was while at the same time giving me some pointers on how I could improve my performance, always the Coach! After that evening, we re-kindled a relationship I cherish to this day, and Coach still comes to my performances whenever we are in the vicinity. Very ready to give a critique, ever the coach.

Coach. Many people have heard or experienced this word in their lives -- basketball, football, track, vocal, I even have a good friend who calls himself a "life coach." There have been several people in my life who have been called by this name, but only one that stands out as a true coach and real mentor; someone who taught me much more about real life than just the fundamentals of a specific sport.

In 1997, so much was going on in my career, touring, awards, gold and platinum albums, it was not often that Coach was at the forefront of my mind. One day my mom called with news that Coach had been in a farm accident and had been severely burned.

He and I had been "hayseeds" all our lives, so the farm accident made sense but the fire part I had a hard time comprehending at first. When mom explained the severity of the situation, I immediately wanted to see him, to be honest, not so much for him but for me.

I dropped everything and drove straight to Ohio and asked mom to call Rosie, Coach's lovely wife, and see if I could visit Jim. I wanted him to know just how important that the life he had led and the small things he did help to shape me into the man I am today.

I was so honored to be able to accompany my father and brother Scott as we went to visit Coach and his wife Rosie in the hospital. Honored to be able to petition our Heavenly Father for the healing of this man and that he would be able to take this tragedy and show Christ's love through all the hurt and pain.

Our great God answered this prayer with a resounding "YES"! I am still amazed and incredibly thankful that God is a God who listens and can bring life out of tragedy.

This book is the story of many people and how Coach impacted their lives, just like mine. Stories of how one "hayseed" allowed the Lord Jesus Christ to speak ever so humbly through him to help mold and redirect the lives of individuals God placed in his life.

I could never be more hopeful and thankful knowing that through this story more lives might be touched just by reading the story of the presence of a man we called "COACH V."

Faith Through Flames

The true events recorded in this book are based on eye-witness accounts, first of an accident that seemed certain to result in death, and then a recovery that can only be called miraculous. The people involved certainly believe it was.

But it's also the story of how a small-town high school football coach encouraged all those around him, not just those who could play for his team. Several of those people played significant roles in his rescue and recovery.

Miracles do happen because the people in this story know they saw one.

CREDITS AND DEDICATION

The cooperation of the **entire VanDeGrift family,** especially **Jim** and **Rosie**, is deeply appreciated. They were willing to share such a personal and prolonged struggle in the hope that others would draw inspiration in times of extreme stress.

They wanted to share the story of a miracle.

Cover design by **Amery VanDeGrift**.

The assistance of **Susan Patterson** and **Linda Oda** and the encouragement of **Marty Roe** and **Ty VanDeGrift**, is gratefully acknowledged, along with everyone who agreed to be interviewed for this project.

This book is dedicated to the abiding faith of Jim and Rosie Van-DeGrift, the VanDeGrift family, and to the people of Lebanon, Ohio who stood with them throughout this ordeal.

CHAPTER 1: AN AUTHENTIC, CARING, GROUNDED MAN

Don't be selfish; don't try to impress others. Be humble, thinking of others as better than yourselves. Don't look out only for your own interests, but take an interest in others, too. – Philippians 2:3-4 (New Living Translation)

This story is about a miracle.

A miracle can mean different things depending on how a person uses the word. Sometimes it describes the joy of a last-second touchdown pass to win the game, or the happy coincidence when a space in a crowded mall parking lot opens at just the right time.

While those things can be pleasant surprises, this story is about the real thing and what it meant to a beloved man named Jim VanDeGrift, his family, and a small Ohio town named Lebanon.

Jim was involved in a horrible accident, a savage fire that seemed to come from nowhere and enveloped him in a flash. It left him with unspeakable pain and wounds that by any known medical standard should have killed him – if not immediately, then certainly within a few hours.

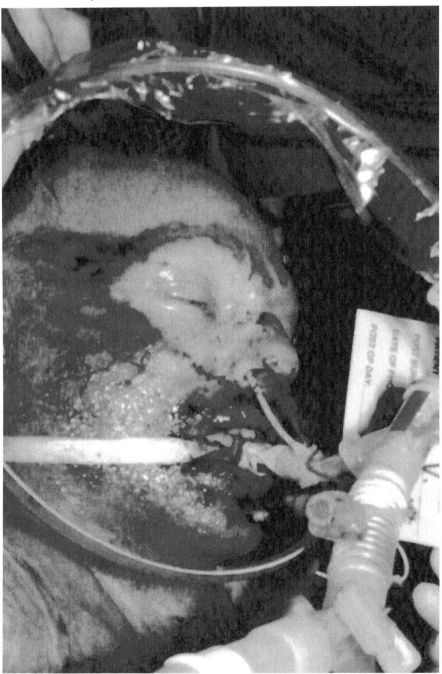

Doctors believed that. They told the family he was going to die. Nearly everyone who knew him in Lebanon, which seemed like the whole town, sadly accepted that they were about to lose him. But as desperately as his family and friends wanted him to live, together they fought through their fears and chose to surrender in faith and accept whatever God chose.

As those around this event came to learn, faith, doubt, and surrender can go hand in hand, and that is why everyone involved in this story will tell you with no prompting that Jim's survival was possible only by God's grace. The VanDeGrift family and the people of Lebanon traveled through darkness that cast deep shadows on each of their souls, and they know what they saw along the way.

That group includes the minister who came to the hospital the night of the fire to offer comfort and went home to begin preparing a funeral service. A nurse who was on duty when the situation seemed beyond medical redemption knew then, and is convinced now, that divine intervention saved his life. Hundreds of people on their knees will tell you they know God heard their pleas.

The family has never tried to guess why their prayers were answered while others offered with the same desperation thousands of times a day in other places for the healing of good people were not. That remains a theological mystery without resolution, except maybe to say Jim's work here wasn't done.

That leads to the bigger story of what impact a life well lived can have. During his working years, Jim was an accomplished high school football coach and administrator. He served on multiple civic boards, was a township trustee, taught Sunday School, and so much more.

When his need was the greatest, the people of his town closed ranks around the man they had known and loved for decades. These were not just former football players, either, because you never had to be an athlete to have worth and potential in Jim's eyes.

He hadn't spent years nurturing only quarterbacks and line-backers, with a sole goal of winning that week's game. He cast a much wider net. He freely gave the gift of encouragement, even when no one was asking. That was especially true for students who might otherwise have been overlooked and left to search in other places for affirmation, belonging and direction.

During the fight for his life and his eventual long-term recovery, many former students sometimes seemed to be divinely placed in his path, almost as if to show the impact a life spent dispensing kindness can have when darkness seemed certain to conquer.

He would tell you that it's a simple thing to build up instead of tear down, and maybe so. But it paid off in ways that could never have been imagined.

Thanks to his encouragement, some students eventually joined the medical field. Others found themselves filling important support roles for their friend and mentor. Another former student, influenced by Jim's belief in him, became the 911 dispatcher who sent the emergency squad speeding to the coach's aid when disaster struck.

Countless others took the lessons he taught them on the ball-fields, and in the hallways of high school into their adult lives. He influenced how they did their jobs, treated their spouses, and raised their families. No one ever wanted to let him down. To do that would be a personal betrayal.

No doubt, there are people like this in villages and towns all around the country. They are this nation's greatest strength.

You know the type – modest, naturally helpful people who never want acclaim. They pitch in because that's what they do. They are happiest when you are happy. A servant's heart beats inside their chest. A higher power guides their steps.

They live by example instead of finger-wagging and preaching.

It's more effective that way. The words have a greater impact because they are offered with compassion.

It starts from the inside. You know that biblical parable about the wise man who built his house on the rock, and how that house withstood life's storm? The metaphorical house Vandy shares with his wife, Rosie, is built upon that rock.

That's true of everyone in the family – from his son Ty, daughters Jami Rotello and Dana Cropper, down through the grandkids. They all talk with God talk a lot, and they talk with each other and pretty much everyone they know about God. No one eats dinner until the food is blessed. On Sunday morning, they're off to church because they would never think of skipping to get a little extra sleep.

They study the Bible. They teach their kids and grandkids about the Bible. They lift each other up. They pray with each other on the phone. They take mission trips. It would be wrong to say they donate hours to the church because that implies it's something they give away from their excess, like taking a box of old clothes to Goodwill. They are servants who live genuine lives. The VanDeGrifts don't just do good things, they are good from the inside out. This family is genuine. The creator of the universe is always in the room, and they believe in his goodness and mercy.

Jim speaks as comfortably about his personal relationship with Jesus Christ as someone else might speak about what they had for lunch. Scores of people attend the Sunday School class he teaches at the local Presbyterian church, and they say it's because he makes things interesting and easy to understand. He brings real-life applications and relevance to his teaching. This authentic man understands his worldly purpose is to be a servant.

He wouldn't admit to anything that noble, of course. He never feels like he does enough. He swats praise like a camper might swat mosquitoes.

Those people make things better. Better? It's more than that. Every town depends on those people who make such a difference no one dares imagine life without them.

They were put here to help. Call it instinct.

Maybe it's the cop whose wise and understanding counsel keeps young ones out of trouble. It might be a special teacher with a gift for helping students see something inside they never knew they had. It could be the pastor with an understanding ear and a voice overflowing with gentle wisdom. Maybe it is a coach who makes raw, undisciplined, and skittish players believe in the unbelievable so that they can achieve the unachievable. Or maybe it's just that nice person who lives down the street, the one with a welcoming smile and a heart that was born to care.

Whatever they do or whoever they are, they are equal parts good and real. They change lives. They don't need a name tag because no one could ever forget them. They're the backbone of the town, and through that, they become its face and voice.

Jim is that indispensable someone. Everyone calls him Vandy or Coach, but a better name is Friend. He is a family man, Christian, confidante, citizen.

He is a man of simple tastes. He likes ice cream, hamburgers off the grill, corn on the cob and fresh-sliced tomatoes. His motto is that every day can be great, but some are better than others. No matter what though, God is good – all the time. Besides his family and God, he loves working, golfing, and going to flea markets. His favorite place to eat is Rosie's kitchen at home, although he will occasionally gather with some guys from the church for breakfast at a local spot. He is a creature of habit, especially during the football season on Friday night, when his favorite hometown team, the Warriors, get ready to play. Chili has to be on the stove, the odor of Rosie's home-cooked delight wafting out the open window and down the driveway as a signal that it's game time.

He has a super-sized soft spot for kids. His youngest daughter,

Dana, still smiles at the memory of how happy he was one Easter when he bought real bunnies for her girls.

There is an admirable consistency about the way he lives, and what you see from day-to-day is what you get. He is an open book with no pretense. Everything is a competition though, even working in the family garden. Who could get the biggest potato?

And heaven help you if Jim picked rotten tomatoes from the fresh, Ohio soil before you did because you would be on the business end of a tomato fight.

Work may be necessary, but there is no reason it can't be fun. It's all in how you approach the job.

Need something? He's all in. Have a problem? He'll be waiting for you inside the house at the end of a steep, narrow and winding hill just outside of town. Relax on his sofa and soak in the view of the dense woods lying just outside the giant picture window. They are a reminder of the cycle of life.

In the summer, those woods spring to rich green, thick with leaves and fireflies, sometimes with the fresh smell left behind after a passing rain. In the winter, they are stark, brown and gothic, sometimes blanketed with traces of snow. On some nights, you might even hear the howling of coyotes on the prowl for fresh game.

Sit down and talk it out over a glass of crisp, cold apple cider. He will listen before he talks, but when the words come, they do so with authority and purpose. He knows what it means to be really alive, and he wants you to have that feeling, too. He knows there is no problem so large that you can't solve it with prayer, faith, sacrifice, and determination to see it through.

CHAPTER 2: A TWIST OF FATE, OR SOMETHING ELSE?

*For I know the plans I have for
you, declares the Lord, plans
for welfare and not for evil, to
give you a future and a hope.
– Jeremiah 29:11 (NLT)*

Jim has been that way for as long as most who knows him can remember. No doubt that traces to his roots in another small Ohio town named Ansonia. When he was growing up in the 1940s and '50s, the place was nothing more than a speck on the map near the Indiana border in west central Ohio, memorable only because Annie Oakley grew up nearby. Ansonia was home to less than a thousand souls then – and not many more now. It covered less than one square mile. The nearby Stillwater River ran past a collection of corn fields and silos wrapped around a few streets that made up the town.

He grew up outside of there in an even smaller cluster of people called Rossburg, just outside of Ansonia. That's where he lived in a five-room house on 160 acres of lush, green Ohio farmland. His mom, Mary Lou, ran the show while Jim's father, Maurice, was gone during weekdays to a carpenter's job about 50 miles away in Dayton, making enough money to pay the bills. The farm gave a lifetime of memories for him and his older siblings – sister, Myra Jean, and brother, Faren.

It was a modest, no-frills upbringing – no TV, no indoor plumbing, and no money to spare. No one seemed to notice.

They had some dairy cows that had to be milked each morning and night, including Christmas, the Fourth of July, birthdays, whatever. Some hogs eventually became breakfast sausage, and chickens for eggs and frying. They grew corn, tomatoes, hay, and other crops. Everyone had chores before and after school – feed the chickens, gather up the eggs to make a little money at the market.

There was a well near the back of the property that pumped enough water for the cattle, so Jim and Faren had the job of driving an old truck out there and filling a giant tank.

The well was by an old sheep shed and a pear tree. One day while Faren watched over the pumping, Jim climbed up on the roof of the shed and pelted his brother with pears – right up the moment when he lost his balance and crashed to the ground.

Broken arm.

Jim's father, a stern, ornery Dutchman with an impulse to reach for the nearest rod lest he spoils the child, would not have been understanding if he knew what happened.

Faren covered for his younger brother, though. Their story was that Jim had fallen out of a swing that hung from the tree branches. OK, maybe it wasn't the truth, but even at that moment, Faren was teaching, as he often did, that while discipline was a hallmark of the family, sometimes it had to be leavened with compassion.

The boys would bulk up their muscles by baling hay; no fancy trips to the gym or the weight room, just ten hours in the broiling summer sun, tossing 90-pound bales into the wagon on the back of the tractor.

Sunday morning was spent in the house of the Lord, of course - a

Methodist church in Rossburg.

Sometimes after church let out, they would get together with some nearby relatives for one of those bodacious Sunday dinners that were an unforgettable and vital part of growing up. They would stuff their faces on food so good it would make your toes curl, and then they'd spend the rest of the day romping and playing, laughing and making memories that can never fade.

There was a time when Jim bought an old Harley-Davidson motorcycle from a neighbor. His parents weren't thrilled, but he rode that bike everywhere – including to his brother's house for a visit.

One day the kickstand slipped down just as he was taking off. Instead of stopping, he tried to reach back with his foot while his hand was revving the throttle.

Mistake.

The motorcycle went out from under its rider, knocking Jim off the seat and he went skidding on the rough pavement. He was wearing Bermuda shorts and no shirt. Bloodied and scratched, he got back on the bike and rode the mile-and-a-half back to the house.

He kept the Harley. He rides a motorcycle today. Don't act surprised.

An upbringing like that might sound like the setting for a Hallmark movie to many. In 1950s rural Ohio, it was a way of life.

Jim was a big man at a small school – there were only 60 or so in his graduating class. He played football in the fall, basketball in the winter, plus baseball and track in the spring. There was no single-sport specialization in those days. If you played one sport, you played them all. He also was in the Future Farmers of America, a class officer, and a student council member. He was on the yearbook staff, the Varsity "A" Club and the Athletic Board.

When he put on shoulder pads and a helmet, he was the type of player he would later love to coach – tough, fearless, and relentlessly competitive. By his senior season, he was co-captain of the team. He played linebacker, offensive line, or anywhere else he was needed. He probably was good enough to attract the eye of schools like Miami of Ohio, Bowling Green, or maybe Ohio University.

"He was a very good football player," teammate Gary Hemmerich said. "He loved football better than anything."

All that went out the window on an October Friday night, circa 1956.

Rival Bradford was walloping Ansonia 35-0 as the first half wound down. Bradford had what politely would be called an over-exuberant team; others might use stronger language. Whatever the case, Ansonia's players were getting hurt, and one of the co-captains had been kicked out of the game. There was no way to close the gap, even with two quarters to play.

How much worse could it get?

They soon found out.

Hemmerich, a sophomore on that team, remembers Vandy was fuming as everyone prepared to meet the coach. They all figured they were due for a severe chewing-out and a challenge to play better in the second half, but instead, he brought some startling news.

What might have seemed like just another mismatch on an obscure field was about to take a twist that would impact hundreds of lives.

"Get on the bus now!"

That was what the coach ordered his team to do.

No one does that.

Was this a bluff to get their attention? Was he serious?

He was.

They were going home, leaving fans bewildered, Bradford's team stunned, and the Ohio High School Athletic Association angry enough to remove the coach by Monday and shut down the remainder of Ansonia's season.

Just like that, young Jim's prep football career was over.

Missing half of his final season should have doomed him to the kind of obscurity reserved for many small-town football heroes who grow older but don't grow up.

It did not. Call it fate if you choose, but it might have just been part of a divine plan.

Unbeknownst to him, Jim's father, Maurice, pleaded with the Ansonia basketball coach to help him get into college somewhere.

They visited West Virginia University, but Jim was too small to play there. Fairmont State, a college in Fairmont, W.V. about two hours south of Pittsburgh, was interested but the feeling wasn't mutual. One of his friends had a sister at Ohio Northern University in Ada, about an hour and a half from Ansonia. That got his attention.

It was a private school operated by the Methodist Church. The school had only a couple thousand students, and Ada wasn't that much bigger than Ansonia. It wasn't big-time football. That's being charitable. At that point, it was really bad football. It was a rare day when the Polar Bears won, but at least Jim might earn a degree, and his career wouldn't end two quarters too soon.

Maybe.

The problem was, Vandy wasn't sure about the whole college scene. He enrolled all right, but after a few practices, he learned that even at that level, college ball was harder than he thought. He was a big man at Ansonia. At Ohio Northern, he was just another freshman getting his head kicked in during practice. He probably wasn't going to play much, either.

There was the school thing, too. Jim was an indifferent student. Football was harder than ever. Nobody at Ohio Northern knew or cared what he had done in high school and retreating to the life he had always known in Ansonia – cows, pigs, chickens, and corn -- was starting to sound pretty good. All of that was on his mind when he came back home for a few days. Why not just stay home and work on the farm? That's what his friends did.

When Jim came home on a short break to visit, his father had an answer in pointed, no-nonsense small-town Ohio talk, and he delivered it during a break on a scorching afternoon. He and his son had been digging a ditch, and Jim was sweating, worn, and ready to do anything but that. The clay was sticking to the shovel, which made the digging even harder.

That's when his father told him to pick that shovel up again.

What?

"Pick it up."

Jim did.

"Make sure you get a good grip on it."

Why?

"If you don't finish school, that's what you'll be holding for the rest of your life. You have a chance for something better."

Message received. Jim left the cows behind and went back to school. It put him on the road to coaching. It put him on the road to Lebanon, thanks in part to a friendship he struck up with another athlete named Ron Holtrey.

Ron and Jim shared common bonds that led to a lifetime friendship. Both had grown up in small Ohio towns. Both had modest financial backgrounds. And both were competitive to the extreme in everything. They shared an off-campus apartment with three other like-minded guys, and something was always going on.

They didn't have a lot of money for socializing, but they did have keys to the school gym. They played basketball late into the night, and the stakes were immense: taunting rights for the winner, humiliation for the loser.

They played badminton, ping-pong, dodge ball -- that game was a killer. Their Wiffle Ball games were epic.

Five years after graduation, Ron came accepted the job as head basketball coach at Lebanon High School. A year later, when the school needed a football coach, he told school board members he knew just the guy to hire. That helped set in motion events that would lift a town and then bring it to its knees when death seemed to come calling.

If he didn't pick up the shovel, or never went to Ohio Northern, or never met Ron Holtrey, who knows what would have happened. Sometimes though, things are just meant to be.

Lebanon school board members believed they were hiring a teacher and a football coach when Jim arrived. They didn't have a clue about the extras that came bundled as a standard part of the package.

Are you looking to get something done for the good of the town? Just tell him what you need. Do you have a friend in a bad way? Do you need a ride? Need a hand? Is someone sick?

Need a place to stay? A bite to eat?

Say the word. If you don't, maybe Jim will figure it out and show up anyway with an aw-shucks smile.

Or maybe it's late at night, and you can't figure out why your world is falling apart. You need to hear someone say it's all going to be OK, so you dial his number. No matter what the clock says, you know he will pick up the phone and stay with you for as long as it takes. You don't quite understand why he cares so much, but he does.

He doesn't play favorites, either. It doesn't matter if you're young or old. Your family doesn't have to be rich. You don't have to be the biggest, fastest, strongest, or smartest.

He will make you feel like he has all the time in the world and has reserved every bit for you. He makes you feel like you matter because, well, you do.

He wants to know how you're doing. Check that. He cares how you're doing. He wants to lift you.

And there's his voice. Time or distance can't dull that sound, heavens no. You can hear it from a thousand miles away. Many still do as it echoes across the decades from high school to gray hair, past distance, time, change, and loss.

It is a cavalry charge of syllables delivered with a commanding, rapid-fire "get-after-it" bark that startles, challenges, or sometimes just plain scares the tar out of you. It remains unchanged despite decades of age. It still is as subtle the locker room speeches Jim used to give to his football players before sending the team out for the homecoming game.

It jolts you out of your easy chair and away from the TV.

He could be asking, well, telling you to do anything.

Take out the trash!

Mow the football field!

Help me paint a house!

Run that extra mile!

Keep going! Don't stop now!

Get over it! Get after it!

Aw, c'mon now, goodness gracious! You can DO this!!

He's not picking on you, not at all. The odds are good he'll be right beside you and pushing himself twice as hard. You, of course, will want to try and keep up. That isn't easy.

Lebanon - or, as locals call it, "Leb-nun" - was just another quaint spot among many idyllic burgs between Cincinnati and Dayton when Jim and Rosie moved there in 1967. About 6,500 people lived there then. It had one high school, a junior high, and three elementary schools – and a harness horse racing track at the Warren County Fairgrounds.

There wasn't much to do then. Many residents drove north about 25 miles to factory jobs in Dayton like National Cash Register or Frigidaire. Or they might commute the same distance to the south for jobs at the General Electric or Ford plants in Cincinnati.

Students got their first part-time jobs at places like the Golden Lamb Inn, the town's landmark restaurant and hotel. Built in 1803, it is the oldest hotel in Ohio, and owners like to brag about how 12 American presidents have visited there. Charles Dickens visited in 1842, but he wasn't impressed.

After asking for a brandy to go with his dinner, Dickens learned the Inn served coffee or tea, no liquor.

It stayed that way until shortly before the VanDeGrifts moved to Lebanon when the Golden Lamb finally obtained a liquor license. Today, it is rock-solid conservative, with a colonial feel and warmth. Republican political candidates regularly stop for speeches, staged  against the Golden Lamb's magnificent colonial architecture for a backdrop.

Its streets, some twisting and others leading up steep hills, are lined with oaks, sycamores, cedars, maples, and pines, and in the fall a visitor might wonder if they have been transported inside a scene by Currier and Ives. When winter brings its razor-sharp, windy bite and blankets of newly fallen snow, those hills transform into something serene and peaceful. No wonder Lebanon has been aptly called a picture postcard town in the national media.

After he became the first man to walk on the moon, astronaut Neil Armstrong settled in Lebanon, on a 300-acre farm not far from the VanDeGrift home and became a low-key part of the community. He wanted to blend in and not have to be a famous intruder.

He came to the right place.

People knew him. They saw him around town, or at the football game, where his son, Rick, was a place-kicker for the Warriors, or the golf course, where he and Vandy frequently played as partners and their families became close friends.

Ty and Mark Armstrong were about the same age and became almost inseparable, running in and out of each other's houses, playing basketball, ping-pong, football, frisbee, you name it. There was fishing in the summer and sledding down snow-covered hills in the winter.

When the weather would oblige, Neil and his wife, Jan, had a regular Friday co-ed golf scramble with Jim and Rosie at the local nine-hole course. Afterward, everyone would gather for a potluck dinner.

"My dad and Jim were very good friends," Mark Armstrong said. "When somebody brings up something about my dad being reclusive, I say no, that wasn't the case. He liked to socialize.

"I think he and Jim hit it off because they were both hard-working and had similar values. They were respectful, patriotic, and loved their country. Both were very down the center line guys. They were both family men, and both had an interest in the community around them."

The locals always said hello, and he returned the greeting. Armstrong even served on the board at the local Countryside YMCA. There were lines people knew not to cross, though.

He wasn't a moonwalker to the people of Lebanon. They didn't pry for tales of Apollo 11 because they knew him as a neighbor and knew when to leave him be. When national media members came around to tell the story of the astronaut living the small-town life, people wouldn't spill a word about their famous friend.

That's Lebanon – small, discreet, protective of its own, even though it had tripled in size from when Vandy arrived. There is only one high school in town though, even though locals identify their heritage by which of the three high school buildings they attended.

The "original" LHS is a grand old structure with narrow hallways and staircases where students sprinted up and down three flights of stairs on their way to class. The largest graduating class was its final one in 1969 – 224 students.

It was also the setting for the movie Harper Valley PTA.

There was the "new" high school on the northern outskirt of town, followed by the "new, new" building they use now.

Growth brought inevitable change. Some of the cornfields around the area have given way to subdivisions filled with upscale homes and parents commuting to executive jobs Cincinnati while their kids shuttle to soccer, football, volleyball or any of the sports of the day.

The essence of Lebanon hasn't changed, though.

Rush hour? That's for big-city folks. You can easily get from one side of town to the other in less than 10 minutes unless the high school homecoming parade has clogged up Broadway heading north from downtown, or the Christmas horse-drawn carriage parade has taken over and brought tens of thousands of visitors to town to soak in its splendor.

But what's the hurry? There is always free parking downtown, so stroll through any of several antique shops or grab a sundae at the Village Ice Cream Parlor. Take a drive along the twisting country roads just outside of town, maybe out to nearby to the ancient Indian burial mounds at Fort Ancient where the Little Miami River, designated a state and national scenic resource, winds toward a merger with the mighty Ohio River east of Cincinnati.

And don't forget autumn Friday nights when the air is crisp and those leaves that offer summer shade turn orange, brown and deep, bright red, raked into piles resembling an artist's palate on yards throughout the town. Corn and beans from the garden are on the stove, apple cider straight from the orchard is on the table, and the marching band is playing Onward Lebanon with all its might.

This is Americana, and that means Lebanon High football. The football stadium now bears Jim's name.

He was the Warriors' head coach for 15 seasons, and he was good. His record was 109-36-8, and his 1980 team made it to the Ohio Class II state championship game. That game did not end well, but after the final gun sounded the mamas and daddies hugged their sons anyway. No regrets. That team had done its best. Besides, getting that far would have been impossible to imagine when Vandy took over.

In 1967, when Jim took over, Lebanon had a sluggish program with few expectations of success. He changed that by making his players understand first how much they mattered and then showing them that losing didn't have to be a way of life.

The great coaches have that gift.

He was a straight-talking rolling ball of knives, too. He set standards and demanded discipline in ways the town had never seen – for players, for cheerleaders, for students, for the guy who worked on his car, for just about everyone.

What no one knew then was that he was hardest on himself.

Dealing with a no-shortcuts coach who looked and acted like a drill sergeant was a culture shock for those who dreamed of being Warriors, but that's how it had to be. Softies don't win championships.

His new team found out immediately how different things were going to be. Vandy was waiting as his players ran down a hill to the field for their first practice. He noticed many of them wore over-sized rubber pads to protect their forearms.

That changed in a hurry. The new coach had a giant cardboard box brought to the field. The practice didn't start until players deposited all those pads into the box.

Part of football in that era meant learning to play with an arm rubbed raw to the point of bleeding by repeated chucks to the blocking sled. He collected the pads. If a player couldn't handle the pain a sled could dish out, how would they do against players from rival teams from Monroe or Franklin?

The arm pads weren't the only thing to go; a lot of other bad habits also were discarded. The Warriors got tougher, and it took only a few years before his teams started winning conference titles with regularity.

Did winning make him a great coach?

Nah.

Lots of coaches win games. On any given Friday night, half the high school coaches in America walk off the field with a victory. Vandy's goal always has been to win life, and games were just part of the toolbox. Sometimes it might have seemed like things were out of order a little, especially after a loss, but Saturday morning would bring the reminder that life always came first.

There was something about him, a quality of leadership that resonated beyond those ten football games in the fall, or the track team he coached in the spring, even though he is in the Ohio High School Hall of Fame for both sports. The force of his personality influenced lives and not just those who played for him.

He filled many roles at the school besides football coach. He was the athletic director, a guidance counselor, a dean, and he taught driver's education. He kept coaching track and cross country after he hung his whistle from football.

He never stopped coaching life.

Jim was always around, mostly in the background. That's how he wanted it -- no fuss, no spotlight, and, please, no credit. It's not about him. It's about you.

That's the message.

For Jim, it was always about someone else – until it wasn't.

That change came on the afternoon of June 5, 1997. That's when everyone was horrified to learn the person who was always there for them might be dead before morning. That's when Lebanon, almost as one, fell to its knees, calling upon deep faith nurtured in many of them since childhood, but also springing to action in a chain of events that revealed the community's abiding deep character and concern for someone else's well-being, developed over decades of looking after each other. It was time to close ranks again, this time around the man who had given so much to them. For once in Vandy's life, it wasn't about someone else.

It was about him, and his townspeople knew who could intercede on his behalf. They made their petitions known to a higher power.

CHAPTER 3: A SPARK, AN EXPLOSION, AND FLAMES

*Give your burdens to the Lord,
and he will take care of you. He
will not permit the godly to slip
and fall. – Psalm 55:22 (NLT)*

It had been one of those fabulous late-spring days in southwest Ohio, a time to be savored because at long last summer was sending signals to set a place at the table because it was coming soon to stay a spell. Winter can drag on forever. Spring can take its sweet time arriving, teasing with alternating days of warming sun, frost and bone-chilling rain.

But when that first real warmth of the season hits with its promise of more to come, it's a time to rejoice. People take off their jackets and sweaters and go outside to smell the grass, once brown and desolate after lying under patches of dirty snow in the winter but now alive, lush and freshly cut. Maybe they venture to the local ballparks to watch the kids play a game.

The temperature had climbed into the mid-'70s, and the sky was flawlessly clear, bright, and blue. Windows were opening in houses all over town. Protective covers were coming off swimming pools, and children chased lightning bugs at night. Picnics, vacations, and parties were on the schedule. Grass and leaves had sprouted on the oak and sycamore trees.

Of course, there was work to be done, but it was all good because it was out in the glorious open air. Recently retired from full-time work with the schools, Vandy was at the wheel of a small, blue Ford 3000 farm tractor as it rumbled along the two lanes of blacktop, curves and rolling hills on State Route 123, pulling a Bush Hog he used to clear some property for a friend in town.

It was around 2 p.m. Jim had finished the job in plenty of time to clean up and keep his tee time with three friends for 18 holes at Holly Hills Golf Club. Perfect.

In a way, though, it was strange. For a while, he had experienced odd feelings at unexpected times when he got to that place along the picturesque stretch of road. He couldn't explain what it was – a foreboding, maybe. It was just something in his mind, a sense something important might happen there.

He was at that spot again, about a mile from his house. Traffic had started backing up behind him, which was strange or maybe a bit of advance Devine intervention because the road is not heavily traveled. Jim became uncomfortable because he didn't like to be in the way, so he maneuvered the slow-moving Ford toward the side of the road and motioned for the trailing cars to pull around.

The tractor was running a little hot; he knew that much. Maybe the cap covering the gas tank was loose. Maybe it was something else. Whatever it was, the cap blew off before he could react, and heated, pungent, foamy gasoline came spraying out of the tank, saturating him and his clothes.

The tractor was picking up speed down a steep drop on the twisting highway. Vandy fumbled for the key to shut off the engine, and that might have caused a spark. Perhaps there was a backfire as the engine stopped. It doesn't matter.

What does matter is that in an instant, the life of one man and one community changed forever.

From that spark, there was an explosion, and instantly the foam erupted into a holocaust of bright, fiery orange flames that quickly left scorch marks some say went 50 feet high up the trunks and branches of some nearby trees. Back on the ground, the fire burned deep into his arms, neck, and face. The force blew him back into his seat. Time stopped.

It's amazing how much information someone can process under stress and maybe all those years on the football sideline making split-second decisions kept him cool. He knew he was on fire but thought that if he jumped back off the tractor, he might land under the Bush Hog. Or the tractor might drift left into oncoming traffic and possibly injure another driver.

Brakes were screeching as people scrambled to help while Jim leaped from the inferno, slamming face-first onto the pavement. Pebbles and dirt dug into the wounds already opening through the blistering, bubbling skin on his face and arms.

Why were all those people there just then on a stretch of road that wasn't heavily traveled? Well, they were.

One man tried to beat the flames with an old blanket he had pulled from his car.

Robert Peeler, a prosecuting attorney who later would become a circuit court judge, rushed to help. He saw a man he couldn't recognize because of the burns rolling on the ground, skin bubbling and melting off his arms in dark gray chunks. In the chaos, that faceless man looked toward the sky and began to shout. What was he saying? Peeler heard the man praying loudly for Jesus to take him home.

That figured. Vandy always told his family and others to be ready with the right answer when it was their time to die. Even in the shock, pain, panic, and frenzied activity from paramedics, there can be clarity which transcends trauma. And at that moment, Vandy accepted that this was his time.

He was ready, even if no one else was.

Peeler rushed to his car and called the Highway Patrol and

looked for a blanket or cold water, anything to douse the flames that were still smoldering on the man. He didn't have either. Later, someone told Peeler that man was Jim VanDeGrift.

Sometimes, the seriousness of events is exaggerated, but not this time. It seemed the only way this story could end was with tears, flowers, and a heartfelt eulogy. That's what everyone who saw him that day and those that followed thought for sure.

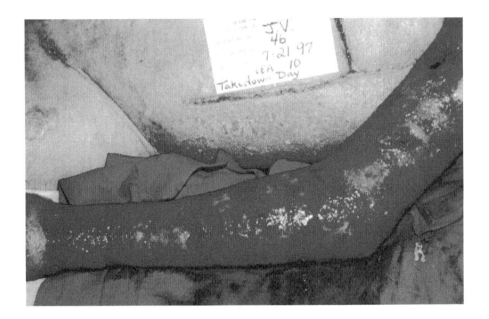

CHAPTER 4: IS MY FACE GONE?

You heard me when I cried, "Listen to my pleading! Hear my cry for help!" Yes, you came when I called; you told me, "Do not fear."
— Lamentations 3: 56-57 (NLT)

Rosie had been at work in the front office at Lebanon High, just a couple of miles away, when Bill Frisch, a Turtlecreek Township road and bridge superintendent, came to the door. He looked anxious. He had just heard over his scanner about an accident involving a tractor and Jim. Did she know anything about it? It sounded bad, but who could say for sure?

Rosie told him that Jim had gone to do some mowing, but ...

Seconds turned to concern, and concern turned to action.

Frisch told her to get in his truck, and as Rosie began to pray as they drove silently. The school was only a couple of minutes from the accident site, and traffic was already backing up. A police officer saw the flashing lights on Frisch's truck, recognized Rosie, and waved them through. No one knows for sure how they'll react to something this extreme. For Rosie, the only way to deal with it was through more prayer.

That's how it had been her life, and it was the foundation of what she and Jim began together when they married on Thanksgiving Day in 1961. She ran the home, and like all coaches' wives, she understood when it was time to be involved, when to take charge, and when to stay out of the way.

Friends knew Rosie as the strength behind the man, and they knew Jim would need every bit of that. She would too.

Medical help was already there when Rosie arrived. EMTs Sandy Stevens and Mike Jameson were working on Jim. Flashing lights were everywhere. A helicopter was on the way from Miami Valley Hospital, about 20 miles to the north. Jim argued with emergency workers who tried to put a breathing tube down his throat, so they gave him a shot to sedate him.

Rosie generally is reserved, preferring to stay in the background, and always to remain calm no matter the circumstance. Even as she prepared to face the unthinkable, she told herself not to go to pieces no matter what she saw. Even as she hurried to her stricken husband, she managed to convince herself she was under control.

But then she saw his skin looked like ashen death. When she touched his head with a reassuring pat, his hair felt crinkly in her hand. The skin on his scorched forearms had already begun to roll.

When Jim told her, "Hey babe, I think my face is gone," Rosie said it wasn't so.

Maybe for the only time in her life, she wasn't telling the truth.

It was gone.

A CareFlight evacuation helicopter kicked up dust and debris as it set down near the stricken coach, and while medical workers tended to her husband, Rosie at that moment became the coach's wife with a to-do list that would bring order to the chaos. It was her defense against panic.

She thought the kids should know first.

Jami was on duty as the executive officer of the 356th Air Reserve Wing at nearby Wright-Patterson Air Force Base in Dayton when her mother called to say she should go to Miami Valley Hospital because dad had been in an accident.

Rosie left out a few details. She didn't tell her daughter that seen him burning on the side of the road. She didn't mention that he had been taken by emergency helicopter to the hospital. Jami was concerned, of course. There didn't seem any reason to believe it was serious, though, her mom had seemed so calm on the phone.

Dana, youngest of the three siblings, was at work in Blue Ash, a Cincinnati suburb about a half-hour to the south, when she got the call. She was surprised to hear her mom at the end of the phone; mom didn't usually call the office.

Rosie repeated what she had told Jami. There has been an accident. Dad's hurt. But then she added that he was being taken to the hospital by CareFlight. Still, she was so calm and matter of fact. Rosie even asked Dana if she could pick up Jami's kids and look after them. That's what seemed so weird as Dana repeated the conversation to a fellow office worker.

But, you don't bring in a medical chopper unless it's serious, do you?

That made sense, of course. What neither Jami nor Dana yet knew was that this was as serious as it gets. Still, what they already knew was unsettling enough. Dana tried to absorb what was happening as she drove home, where a message was waiting on her answering machine. Because Lebanon is a small town, news travels quickly, and friends already had put things into motion. Don't worry about Jami's girls, the message said.

A friend from her Bible study group stepped up to take care of them.

Ginny Kuntz, a close family friend, heard what happened and went to the Presbyterian Church building and knelt in a pew, asking for God's guidance. She was led to call Dana and offer a ride to the hospital. Blessings can come in unexpected ways. Dana wasn't all that sure how to get there, so was grateful to accept.

Rosie got there with an assist from Lee Day, another close friend. As he drove her up Interstate 75 toward Dayton and the hospital, she prayed for calm and strength. Jim needed her. The kids needed her. Friends would need her. And she would need them, more than she could imagine.

CHAPTER 5: DAD'S HURT

I have told you all this so that you may have peace in me. Here on earth you will have many trials and sorrows. But take heart, because I have overcome the world. – John 16:33 (NLT)

Dana was set back by the size of the crowd already at the hospital when she arrived. The hallways leading to where her father lay were already filling to overflow as friends and neighbors dropped what they were doing to be there with their friend.

She got a glimpse of a body that doctors had pushed into the hallway on a gurney, wrapped in gauze, with a grotesquely swollen head that Dana thought looked like a watermelon. No one told her it was her father, but one glimpse of his big toe and she knew. For a family so used to being in control, the uncertainty was terrifying.

Ty, oldest of the three, was in Valrico, Florida, a suburb east of Tampa. His wife, Mary, answered a call from a friend asking, "Do you know something about Mr. VanDeGrift being burned by a tractor?"

What was it? How bad? Hard to tell.

After Ty eventually reached his mother, he initially was left with the same uncertainty about what was happening. Even as she said it might be serious, Rosie's voice didn't betray any of the fear that was beginning to overtake her. She told Ty not to rush up; maybe wait until tomorrow when they would know more. She promised to keep him posted. There wasn't much more she could say.

Minutes can seem like days when waiting for news at a time like this. Inside the hospital, the three VanDeGrift women and their friends talked. They held hands. Sometimes they laughed. They waited. They prayed. They waited. They tried to keep each other calm, even as their hearts were pounding.

They called upon every Bible verse and Sunday School lesson they had ever known. They grew up learning about faith, but it was time to live it. It was time to let go, let God. Those are easy words to say when you're not staring into an uncertain abyss. It's much harder when your mind is telling you this can't be happening, but the other part of you is arguing that it will be all right because it has to be because that's Gods' promise spelled out in the Bible.

If you pray to God in the name of his son, and you accept the words written in the book of Hebrews – that faith is the assurance of things hoped for, proof of things not seen – then God will hear you. It's the rock believers hold in the storm.

Of course, it was bad, but God was in the room, and He would use the doctors to fix everything. At that moment, those aren't just words from an ancient text. They are a lifeline, and ben a power greater than themselves was all any of them had.

Rosie had been waiting nervously with her daughters and maybe a dozen other men, friends of Vandy, in a long rectangular room. A doctor entered as Dana and Jami flanked their mother. Jami remembers he started "spitting out all this stuff" that was hard to process, at least until he made it unmistakably clear what was going on.

"The next few hours are going to be critical," he told them. "Hopefully we still have him by morning."

Hopefully?

It was like a force had reached into Rosie's body and savagely yanked the breath out of her. She struggled to find her thoughts because these thoughts were unthinkable. There was a momentary silence before she uttered, "Say that again?"

Her husband had second- and third-degree burns over more than 80 percent of his body. His face, arms, hands, and legs were badly damaged. Some of the burns had gone deep into the muscle.

"What does that mean?" she asked.

It meant that the man of medicine, in his detached way, was preparing Rosie for Jim's certain death.

There is a formula called the morbidity ratio, the doctor explained clinically, to determine the chances of survival. Take the person's age and add it to the percentage of burns. The higher the total, the less likely they will live. If it's 100 or more, there is no chance.

Jim was 58 years old, with burns over 82 percent of his body.

His total was 140.

By any human knowledge, he faced imminent death.

In that instant, there was no hiding behind denials any longer. The dam holding in Rosie's reserve and unspoken fears shattered, releasing them from the place she had kept them sealed in the deepest recesses of her being and they flooded every fiber of her body.

Trembling, she almost forced the words from her mouth.

"Are you saying he could die?"

"It's touch and go," the doctor told her.

Touch and go? What does that mean?

With crushing finality, the doctor told her it meant her husband was going to die. He had almost no chance of survival. He told her that if there is anyone she needed to call, she should do it now, and that person had better hurry. Her husband was slipping away, almost the point of no return. The doctor said they hoped to keep Vandy alive at least until morning, but she likely soon would be a widow.

For the first time since she heard about the accident and said her prayers to God, and she saw her husband on the side of the road as she fudged the truth about his face, Rosie fell to pieces. The terror she had fought to suppress pushed past her defenses. To Dana, it seemed like her mother's despair had turned to desperate, heaving groans.

Ooooooh ..... ohhhhhh.

At that moment, when a stray spark from a tractor had sent the wonderful life Rosie had known into terrifying disarray, she did the only thing she knew how to do – the only thing left to do.

She fell to her knees.

Everyone with her did the same.

People just kept coming to the hospital, but why? Prayer was all anyone could offer at that point, and they could have done that anywhere. People had to come through. In these hours of desperation, they were drawn by instinct to surround the coach and his family with love. Some were close friends from the church like Rev. Dr. Bill Cain, pastor of the Presbyterian Church where the VanDeGrift family worshiped.

Cain went speeding up Interstate 75 to be with his stricken friend and to minister to the family as soon as he received the call about what happened.

He was familiar with death and recognized it as an intensely private, sacred time. He had held the hands of those about to die. He has witnessed death in the faces of the faithful in their final moments. He had offered comfort to families paralyzed by fear and grief. He had heard their cries and seen their tears. He knew all the signs, almost as clearly as if death had a face as it stood to wait inside the room for the final moment.

He saw death in the hospital that night.

He saw it so clearly that his mind shifted from prayers for heal-ing to a plea for God to make Vandy's passage go easily. There was nothing else that could be done for the coach, and Cain wasn't concerned for his friend's soul; he knew Vandy would soon meet Jesus face-to-face. The greater concern was for Rosie and the family. They would need him the most.

Cain knew the funeral service would be a large one. People would come from everywhere to say goodbye to a friend they loved and admired. The number of mourners might overwhelm church capacity, and he had to be ready. More importantly, given the nature of what had happened, the family would need every bit of spiritual nourishment he could provide.

Cain was thinking all those things after he drove home from the hospital. And around 1:30 a.m., wired and unable sleep, he began to write a farewell funeral message for Jim.

Ty had arrived nearly two hours earlier after receiving a call from his mother that waiting was not an option.

There was the rush to the airport in Tampa to catch an AirTran flight to Dayton, which led to a frenzied 6-minute dash through the Atlanta airport to make the connection. Flight attendants kept the cabin door open while he sprinted down the jetway. Everything was a blur.

There was the ride from the Dayton airport, where two of Ty's friends from high school – Craig Colston and Troy Holtrey – were waiting to pick him up.

After he threw his hastily packed duffel bag into the trunk, Ty sat in the front while Craig, at the wheel, flew south 15 miles down Interstate 75 toward the hospital. The drive only took a few minutes, but it seemed much longer. Moments of thick, painful silence, partly from exhaustion and partly from shock, were occasionally punctuated when Craig would begin talking animatedly about how serious this was and Jim might not make it, and ...

And what?

Ty, whose career is leading and controlling as a national business development leader for a global accounting and consulting firm, is used to being in charge, and that means sorting through speculation and getting to the facts. Guessing is not part of the equation.

It was nearly midnight when the car sped into the parking lot at the hospital, but that didn't matter. Ty was wide awake because the adrenaline was thundering through his veins. He was finally going to get some answers to a drama that began eight hours and nearly a thousand miles ago.

That occupied his mind as they got out of the car and headed toward the hospital door, but even with that he couldn't help but notice the size of the crowd of people still gathered outside the building, even at that late hour. There were many familiar faces, and almost everyone was praying, but it sounded like a single voice too loud to ignore.

"Dear Lord ... we lift up our friend and brother ...

"Lord ... we pray for your healing power ...

"Father God ..."

That's when it hit Ty. Those people weren't just praying; they were pleading with God to save the life of his father, the indestructible person, and coach who had taught him how to be a quarterback, a leader, and a man.

It was extraordinary. Ty had never seen anything quite like this, but it was only beginning.

As he made his way past the praying crowd outside and through the door, he encountered dozens of more people crowding the narrow hallways leading to the emergency room and praying constantly. Praying and pleading with God to keep their friend alive.

How bad was this anyway?

One look at all of the medical people working feverishly on the unidentified, bloated body inside the intensive care room gave Ty that answer.

Faith, as everyone learned that night, does not mean the absence of uncertainty. In many ways, it is an act of individual surrender to God, knowing the odds, yet putting the power of all the years of listening and absorbing sermons, Bible studies, Sunday School classes, and home groups into action. It was the moment when you pray because that's all that is left, and you surrender out of trust that God won't abandon you when you need him most.

For those outside and looking through the thick glass of the intensive care unit window, it was sickening. They could see endless loops of protective gauze wrapped mummy-like over and around his body. Tubes carried medication into him, and a tracheotomy helped him breathe. Doctors sliced incisions in the shape of a goalpost deep along the sides of his chest to ease the pressure on his swollen skull. While the doctors worked feverishly, all anyone else could do was wait in the silence so thick it was almost stifling.

Tom Hoverman and his wife, Kristie, caught glimpses of the stricken coach. The Hovermans knew him as few others did. Tom served as an assistant football coach with him for many years, including eight seasons as defensive coordinator. He succeeded Vandy as the Warriors' head coach in 1982.

Kristie was a student and cheerleader at Lebanon High when Vandy arrived. Over the years she learned to grow comfortable with calling him "Jim" instead of Mr. VanDeGrift, but it wasn't easy. Her experience as a coach's wife and being so close to the action helped forge a deep, special relationship with the man who was fighting for his life.

As the long minutes of the emerging nightmare dragged on, Kristie remembered thinking how awful it would be for Rosie to be alone just when the couple's kids were grown, and they had time for each other.

So, what to do?

Surrender in love.

Prayers had been offered, and there would be more. Whether their friend would live or die was something over which they had no control. What they could do was pray and believe that God was listening.

Tom Russell, who played football for Jim and later was on his coaching staff, told his wife that night that he wasn't sure coach was going to make it. He told her prayer was the only thing that would save their friend.

There is no numbering the prayers offered that night. They came from outside the thick glass window of the intensive care unit where doctors and nurses worked to save him. They came from the hospital chapel, and they continued from the parking lot. There were former football players and coaches. Others knew Jim only as a friend, not a coach. Lebanon had entered the valley of the shadow, knocked to its knees, and the people knew only one way out.

The people spontaneously sang the traditional hymns of faith, timeless words of hope inspiration like "I come to the garden alone" and "Amazing grace, how sweet the sound."

The family was staggering under the blow their father and patriarch had been dealt. The lessons they had learned through life were about to put to a defining test, and it's no shame to admit they were afraid because darkness was closing in, and there was no promise of light.

In those desperate hours, they would lift each other. No matter the outcome, they would not stray from the rock upon which their life is founded. These weren't theoretical lessons in a Sunday School class any longer; they were lifelines. They would choose belief in the face of fear and trust under the deepening shadow of the valley.

There would be no sleep that night. People were overwhelmed, wrung out, and too exhausted even to cry.

That might have been the longest night of any of their lives as they looked up from the valley of fear and pain, but the night always ends with the dawn.

And somewhere in the depth of that darkest night, Vandy had a vision. It wasn't the bright light some have reported from near-death experiences. He did not see Jesus, asking if he wanted to stay or go.

What he saw and felt was pure evil.

Faceless specters that carried guns were attacking him. All he had was a 2-by-4 piece of board to fend them off. He kept running, and they kept chasing.

Was he running out of fear?

No. Jim knew that if he died at that moment, heaven would be his next stop.

Survival instinct?

Maybe. Even that has its limits though.

Near exhaustion in his dream, he finally emerged from a hiding place behind a wall by railroad tracks and screamed at his tormentors to finish the job. Just shoot me!

There was something else, though – a different feeling, like someone was keeping the evil away. Jim couldn't explain what that was, but that presence was there, a force that even in the valley of the shadow of death wouldn't let evil have the final say.

And when the sun broke through the darkness over Miami Valley Hospital the next morning, Jim was still alive.

Joe Henderson

It was a start.

They were down, but collectively they would rise because no matter the score or circumstance, VanDeGrifts do not quit.

CHAPTER 6: ONE DATE

Who can find a virtuous and capable wife? She is more precious than rubies. – Proverbs 31:10 (NLT)

The union between Rosalie Rehmert and the overly confident young man from Rossburg named Jim VanDeGrift nearly ended before it had a chance to start. For that, go back to a Saturday night in Frenchtown, Ohio, which isn't a town at all. It's at most a spot on the road, two exit signs up from nowhere.

Years before, for reasons that probably made sense at the time, someone built a dancehall there named The Crystal Ball. The big bands of the era like Guy Lombardo, Stan Kenton, and others had come there to play. And it's where the young lady her friends called Rosie had gone with girlfriends.

The daughter of deaf-mute parents, she was raised on a 60-acre farm near Greenville, Ohio with six siblings who closely supported each other throughout their lives. There were cows and pigs, corn, soybeans, wheat, and beans, and everyone joined in to help. That's how they do it on the farm in Ohio. Everybody does their part because the family depends on it. She learned how to butcher the animals and how to can vegetables and meat for the winter.

But on this night, she was in Frenchtown to listen to some music, maybe dance a little, kick back, and have some fun. A strapping lad with the most remarkable blue eyes she had ever seen approached her table and asked if she wanted to dance. He stood about 6-foot-1, weighed about 225 pounds. He had a thin, blond mustache, blond hair cut in a flattop, and a way about him that seemed to shout he wasn't afraid of anything.

When they got to the floor, though, he just stood there with his arms draped over her shoulders. He wasn't moving. He certainly wasn't dancing. What was going on? This wasn't normal. He kept glancing back over his shoulder with a snarky little grin. The song played on, but his legs stayed planted like a stalk of Ohio corn.

It was all about a bet.

A bunch of the guys saw Rosie from across the room. She was a 19-year-old beauty, about 5-foot-4, with her hair stylishly in a French Twist. He had bragged he could get any girl in the joint to dance with him. Oh yeah? Think so? What about that good-lookin' girl over there? Never gonna happen!

Jim was never one to back away from a challenge.

What price victory, though? After all, what he did probably should have earned a Coca-Cola thrown in his face and the end of a not-so-beautiful non-friendship.

Boy meets girl; boy makes the girl feel like a stuffed animal he won at the county fair. Then the girl tells the boy to take a long leap off a short pier. Strange thing, though. The brash boy with the curious dancing style kept hanging around that night. The more he talked, the less impressed Rosie became. He seemed to be stuck in one direction – forward.

Could he take her home that night, he asked?

"No."

"OK, how about a date tomorrow night?"

"No."

"Why?"

She had to work.

The persistent young man at her side was dubious.

"Work on a Sunday night? Nobody does that."

She was a long-distance operator at the phone company, she explained. People liked to make a lot of calls on Sunday night. She didn't get off until 10 p.m. They couldn't go out.

What part of "no" wasn't sinking in here? What Rosie didn't understand, though, is what guys will do when they are smitten. And so, as she walked to her car the following night after her shift ended at the phone company, she heard a whistle.

She turned her head and saw her not-so-dancing partner grinning from his car.

You really do work late, the dashing young man with the light blue eyes told her.

"Yes."

OK, he said, how about we go out later this week, maybe to the Darke County Fair. Bad idea. The fair is not a place you go for a date. The fair is where you go to meet people, hang with friends, see and be seen, do silly stuff.

She said no.

Jim does not discourage easily. He managed to "accidentally" bump into her every night that week at the fair. What was happening? He may not have known it at the time, and certainly, Rosie didn't, but Jim knew she was something special.

They talked, a little at a time. Rose discovered Jim was a football player. Like her, he grew up on a farm. He was kind of cute, you know. It was those eyes. And at some point, under the twinkling lights and carnival sounds at the fair, he managed to get her to say yes to a date.

One date.

What's the harm with one date?

Even then, she wasn't convinced. She needed a scouting report. Her brother was dating a girl who had gone out with Jim. What did she think of him?

Not much. He's too cocky.

She already was skeptical about this, and the ex-girlfriend didn't help, but a promise is a promise. She kept the date.

One date.

Surely, that's where it would end. They went to a drive-in movie. Rosie was expecting more of the same from the aggressive young fellow who wouldn't take no for an answer, but that's not who she went out with that night.

Instead, she discovered another side of his personality. He was polite, respectful, the perfect gentleman. They talked throughout the movie, and he seemed to listen when Rosie was speaking. He didn't smoke or drink, either. She liked that.

He was a Christian, too. She really liked that.

He couldn't tell her the moment, the hour, or even the day he was saved – probably because there was never going to be another way. Jesus was in control of his life. As he would put it, "I just always felt a need to do good things."

He was leaving for Ohio Northern University to start his junior year, and summer football practice soon was about to begin. Would she write to him there?

She teased him.

Sure, she would write. All Jim had to do was write to her first.

Here we go again – back on the dance floor. Who will blink?

No way, Jim said. Here are the rules: She had to write the first letter.

Rosie told him to keep dreaming. He was shaking his head, no. Something was going on here, though – the beginnings of something neither of them knew at that moment. Keep dreaming?

She didn't know he was already dreaming about her.

Just maybe, she was doing a little dreaming too.

Days later, she got a letter with an Ada, Ohio postmark – home of Ohio Northern University.

Her young man had blinked.

He scribbled, "If you can take time out from your busy schedule, please drop me a line."

She took out a piece of paper.

"I'm taking time out from my busy schedule to drop you a line," she wrote. She then drew a line down the middle of the paper to the bottom and signed her name. She had done what he asked. She dropped him a line.

Players were gathering around the training table to eat when mail call arrived. Getting a letter from a girl was a big deal – especially at the end of football practice when you're sore, worn out, recovering from an afternoon the scorching sun, and all you have for company is a hundred guys and a bunch of screaming coaches.

Moments like these are gold. They are to be shared to lighten life that is summer two-a-days.

So, the guys gathered around, some standing on chairs to get a better look and maybe share a vicarious escape as Vandy triumphantly opened the letter. Was it a love letter? Was it mushy? C'mon man, READ IT OUT LOUD!

That's when they saw the line.

She dropped him a line, all right.

Football players can be sooooo understanding. First one guy laughed, then another, and another, and before long the laughter echoed and caromed off the walls and landed squarely on Jim's flushed, sputtering face. There was nothing he could do but sit there and take it.

Once again, it might have been the end of a friendship that was off to a sputtering start. That line in Rosie's letter may as well have been the line you don't cross, the one that marks the boundary of a young man's frail and still-developing ego.

But a day or so later, he got another letter. This one had actual words. Nice words that carried the hope that maybe this might work out after all.

And, well, OK, she was forgiven – just this once. So it went. Back and forth, words on paper, thoughts expressed, dreams taking shape. Someone along the way, it hit them both. They had found their dance partner.

You don't rush into these things, though. Jim wasn't interested in anyone else, and Rosie started to think he was her man, and they talked about getting married one day, but who knows? Talking about maybe, possibly, one day joining up doesn't count as a proposal. That didn't come for about two more years after they first met.

He had graduated from college and was an assistant football coach at Marysville High. It was another small town, and he had a job to do and players to coach, and while he had realized this would be his life's work, there were also lots of empty hours in a place where he didn't know a lot of people. It gave him time to think about Rosie.

Rosie.

She would visit him there on Friday nights, staying with the family of another coach, but it wasn't enough. He had grown up in a family, and he wanted a family of his own. He was a young man on the way up, a college graduate with responsibilities and plans. Rosie was part of this plan because when you have something this good, better keep her. He wanted Rosie beside him until death they do part.

Small technicality: Before any of that could happen, he had to tell her so.

The proposal came tumbling out on a late October night like someone trying to schedule a meeting. There was no moonlight stroll along a lake. He didn't get down on one knee. There was a football season to finish, and, well, here goes.

He was direct and to the point, like someone sending in a play from the sideline.

Hey, he said. Let's get married over Thanksgiving. Whaddya think?

That was about three weeks away.

What did she think? Are you kidding?

It wasn't flowers and candy, or some other fairy tale proposal Rosie had dreamed about, but it didn't matter. She had often asked God to send her the right man to marry, and now, God had done his part. All she had to say was yes.

On November 18, 1961, she received an engagement ring for a birthday present.

On November 23, at St. John's Lutheran Church in Greenville, as family members looked on, Jim took her hand, she took him, and two became one. Over at the reception, they all had a piece of wedding cake.

Rosie had baked it.

Her name now was Rosie VanDeGrift, and she was a coach's wife along with everything that meant.

Joe Henderson

CHAPTER 7:
SURRENDERING IN FAITH

My son, pay attention to me and watch closely what I do. – Proverbs 23:26 (New Century Version)

Ty was the first of their three children and the only boy they would have. He made quite an entrance into the world. Jim and Rosie were just days from moving to Chillicothe after he had been named head coach at Unioto High School. The problem was, head coaches are supposed to have detailed notebooks typed out for how they want to run their program.

Jim didn't have one.

So, on the hottest night of the summer, Rosie, nine months pregnant, typed page after page of the coaching book for her husband. Her reward was a trip to Dairy Queen.

And contractions.

She made it through the night, but by the next morning, it was time to go to the hospital. The problem was, Vandy committed to teaching a driver's education class. He told Rosie to hang tight while he picked up the Chevy Impala at the school, then showed up back at the house with four students in tow. Rosie scooted in as best she could, and one of the most unusual birthing stories was underway.

Remember, this was 1963, and roles were a little different then. The hospital labor room was basically a giant dorm where expectant mothers were separated only by a hanging sheet. Fathers were not expected to be part of the scene, so Vandy sized everything up – many women in various stages of labor, screaming in that special kind of agony only mothers can fully appreciate, many of them using words you don't say in church.

Time to go.

He patted Rosie on her protruding belly and said something like, "Let me know when it's over." He went back to school, and then home – getting occasional updates until finally, praise be and congratulations! You have a son!

As Ty discovered, a boy in the VanDeGrift house was going to grow up around football, no questions asked. Fortunately, it didn't take much convincing. He would learn what Friday night meant, and he would understand what it took to prepare for those games. Ty proved to be an eager study. By the fourth grade, he was the starting quarterback for one of the Lebanon pee-wee teams. He wasn't big then.

That didn't change much.

He grew to maybe 6-feet tall if you stretched him tight from head to toe. He weighed about 180 pounds, with a thick, almost stumpy physique. That's not supposed to be big enough to start at any position on a lot of good high school teams, let alone quarterback.

There he was, though, barking signals for a team that went to the state final. He played so well that he became Lebanon's first quarterback to be chosen all-state. What he lacked in size, he more than made up for in drive, determination, smarts and an indisputable command of the huddle. He was in charge.

He had his father's voice and limitless enthusiasm. Whatever he did, he believed he could always do it better the next time. Whatever the game, Ty believed he could win. Challenges were simply problems he hadn't yet conquered. That was the way of life.

After leaving the Lebanon cocoon, Ty took a full college scholarship, and he had an outstanding freshman year as the starting quarterback for Georgetown. A year later, it looked like it might end the way a lot of football careers do, with a blown-out knee that required complete reconstruction. But that knee belonged to Ty VanDeGrift, and he wasn't about to let it get in the way of football.

Maybe it was genes, or maybe the echo of his father's voice drove Ty through the tortuous rehabilitation to get back on the field. But he made it.

Think he was in the right place? While his football talent and competitive drive attracted the attention of Big Ten coaches, at Georgetown, he met a wonderful lass named Mary Collins from nearby Lexington. She had a certain way about her, with an inner strength and faith that ran deep.

They were perfect for each other.

All that and more is what Rosie signed up for when she said, "I do." Her husband might have a servant's heart, but he is competitive to the max, and Jim passed that on to his son. Both of them don't simply want to win; they must win at everything, from Friday night football to a round of golf with friends or each other. The golf course became an outdoor classroom, where a father taught his son to be ready for the day when it would be his turn to teach. You don't just play. You play to win. More to the point, make sure you don't lose and learn to handle the pressure, tune out distractions, and realize what's at stake. Learn what only those truly committed to a life of competition understand.

Losing could make you sick. No, that's not quite right. Losing should make you sick. Losing should ruin your day. Losing is what the other guy does, and it must be avoided through work, attention to detail, and understanding no individual is bigger than the team. Channel everything into a group effort.

Winning begins on the inside, though.

If you missed the putt, you better not make an excuse, and heaven help you if a cuss word escaped your lips. It wasn't God's fault that the putt rolled past the hole; it was yours. If there was blame, then point the finger first at yourself and then get better. If you fell, GET UP!

Ty always did.

He learned his lessons well.

CHAPTER 8: THE MIDDLE CHILD

Children are a gift from the Lord. – Psalm 127:3 (NLT)

Jami was next.

Sure, it was a kneejerk over-reaction when Jim said almost in jest to "put it back!" after he learned his second child was a girl. Jim was a bit a chauvinist, you know, and Jami didn't come into the world until 1965. Such attitudes might have seemed standard for males in the '50s, but times were a'changin'.

The women in the front office at his high school certainly weren't amused, and they decorated the mailbox at his home in pink ribbons and balloons to make sure he got the message.

Jim wanted a large family, all boys. Eleven sounded like a good number, just enough for a VanDeGrift football team. But, the best coaches can make quick adjustments, and Jim did that with the little girl who had entered his well-ordered life. Jami was here. She wasn't going back, so she would play as large a part in the VanDeGrift family game plan as her brother Ty.

That was just fine with Jami. She adored her father. She loved that the life he lived at home was the same as the one he lived Sunday at church.

She loved that he was the head football coach of the high school she attended.

She was thrilled to be included when her mother, brother, and father went on a mission trip to Haiti when she was 14.

Why Haiti?

Because Jesus Christ is real, and the family was led by Him to go there.

It was the first time she had been on an airplane. Once they landed at the tiny Port Au Prince airport, she spent two weeks sewing clothes for people in need while Ty and her father helped build a church. Rosie taught villagers songs.

It was a life-changing experience.

"I remember sitting outside, trying to converse with the kids," she said. "They wanted to touch me. The people were not just happy. They were smiling from the inside. Their smiles were intentional. They needed so much, but this was authentic Christianity. They just needed to see Jesus with skin on. They loved Jesus."

Everything she saw spoke of God, service, honesty, and hard work. And there was that time at a Fellowship of Christian Athletes meeting when her dad asked everyone, "If you died tonight, where would you go?"

In that family, knowing the answer was their core value and comfort in the trial by fire that was to come.

A girl in the VanDeGrift family didn't receive special breaks. That meant getting to bed early even on a Friday night because, as Jim liked to tell his kids, you can't hoot with the owls and still soar with the eagles. The eagles were soaring by 7 a.m. Saturday. It started with an eyeball-awakening pounding on the bedroom door.

Get up!

Get to work! You're wasting daylight!

In this family, there is no such thing as halfway or lowering of expectations.

"I always wanted to impress Dad," she said. "I might get kind of a smile or a head nod, but I knew that was approval, and it meant the world to me. That's just the way my dad was. There was always something you could do better. That didn't upset me because I knew he lived it."

They might mow the grounds at one of the local cemeteries, or work in the garden, or, oh, who knows what else. Maybe paint a sign or dig sweet potatoes. There were always things to do, and when Jami wasn't handling chores at home, there was distance running to do the cross country and track teams, or varsity cheerleader practice.

Typical VanDeGrift: Jami would finish a long cheerleading workout, then lace up her Pumas for a 4-mile training run up and down those rolling southwest Ohio hills as she headed toward home. Those were good things at the moment that built self-discipline, of course, but Jim was always thinking ahead. There was college to plan for and the VanDeGrifts, living on a school-system salary, weren't wealthy people.

"He used to tell me, 'Cheerleading isn't going to pay your way through college,'" Jami said.

She thought she had that problem solved after she earned an ROTC scholarship to the University of Tennessee – tuition paid, and her future committed to the military. That was the plan, at least until she answered the phone in the family home shortly after graduating from high school.

The caller on the other end asked her to hold please for Congressman Bob McEwen.

"Jami?"

"Yes."

"This is Congressman McEwen. We want to congratulate you on your appointment to the Air Force Academy."

She had applied to the Academy, mostly out of a wild hair she had to try something different and take a shot – never dreaming she would be accepted. Maybe the letter of recommendation from their neighbor, Neil Armstrong, helped her move up the list.

Maybe it was something else.

"I believe he helped, but God made it happen," she said. "God opened the door. I just walked through it."

Jami started screaming after she hung up the phone from the congratulatory call. Rosie dropped a broom she was using to sweep the floor and ran across the kitchen to hug the newest U.S. Air Force cadet. Three weeks later, Jami was driven to the Dayton airport by her parents and boarded a plane for Colorado Springs.

It was Jami's turn in the spotlight.

She became a pilot, soaring with the eagles, and reached the rank of Lt. Colonel before retiring after 28 years. But before that, she was … wait for it …

A cheerleader for the Air Force football team.

Well, that and a golfer.

When Jami arrived at the Academy, the women's golf team needed players. She had only been golfing a handful of times with her father. He taught her how to hold the club, drive the cart, and keep score. But Division I intercollegiate golf?

"We weren't allowed to call home often, but I didn't have any golf clubs, and this thing came up with the team, so they let me," she said. "I told dad about the team, and the next thing I know I get the mail, and it's a set of golf clubs. And mom sent me some cute outfits."

She still had to try out, but the shortage of players – and she was sort of one - made that a technicality.

"I don't think the coach thought too much of me," she said.

"We'd go out sometimes to play, and he'd say, 'Um, VanDeGrift, you will just caddy with me today.'"

But there was cheerleading, and that meant traveling to football games at places like Notre Dame, Navy, and Army – close enough that her mom and dad could come and watch her cheer on the sidelines.

Funny how that worked out.

She met the love of her life in the Air Force, a dashing young man named Tom Rotello, coming out the locker room after a football game at Notre Dame – tired, pale, and headed for the team bus. He was a starter on the football team, one of the Academy's best players, all-conference. And as Jami learned after they began to date, he met the criteria – football, family, and deep faith.

When Tom formally proposed to Jami, at the VanDeGrift home no less, he did it the old-fashioned way – asking Vandy first for his daughter's hand.

CHAPTER 9: THE YOUNGEST DAUGHTER

*I could have no greater joy
than to hear such things
about my children. – 3 John
1:4 (New Living Bible)*

Dana entered the world nine years after Ty and seven years after Jami. Her birth was something of an adventure. It had started as a nice early spring day, and Rosie, nine months pregnant, spent much of it planting a garden with Ty and Jami.

Jim stayed busy helping build a barn on their property. He even thought about joining Tom Hoverman on a short trip to look at a motorcycle, but that idea got squelched in a hurry when, around 5 p.m., Rosie said, "Um, I'm having contractions."

About four hours later, it was time to go to a hospital in Kettering, about 20 miles to the north. Things had gotten complicated, though. Ohio weather can abruptly change, and the nice day had given way to sleet and freezing rain that covered the roads and the car windshield in sheets of ice.

They made it safely through, and around 1 a.m. Dana entered the world. Given the gap in their ages, it does not surprise that her experiences while growing up were much different from her older siblings.

For one thing, her father had stopped coaching football long before she entered high school, so her memory of his coaching years wasn't so much about competition as it was the aroma.

You see, there were a couple of ways Dana, knew it was football season.

When the assistant coaches gathered at the house for meetings during the week, she and Jami had the job of bringing snacks or "Victory Treats" her mother had prepared to the basement while the staff studied film and did football stuff. If that wasn't proof enough, she could smell football on Friday night.

Well, technically, not football.

But when she got off the school bus and headed up the steep, twisting driveway to the house, the distinct odor of her mother's homemade chili came wafting out the doorway.

Dad always insisted on chili on Friday night before a game.

Rosie made the good old-fashioned kind – ground beef, beans, tomatoes she had canned from the garden, nice and spicy. Had to have it. It was one of those silly rituals some coaches go through when getting ready to play, except it wasn't silly.

It was important.

Game tape?

Check.

Players dressed and ready?

Check.

Bowl of chili?

Check. Game on.

But that's where Dana's experience as the coach's kid ended. By the time she was in high school, another man was coaching the football team, and her father was in the front office as athletic director, an administrator who could (and did) tell students what to do.

She didn't catch any breaks there. Big surprise, right?

There was the time when she was a senior and was hauled out of class to meet with the counselor – her father. There was an underclassman who was upset that seniors called him by a nickname he didn't consider flattering.

Jim demanded to know if Dana knew his real name.

She did not.

"Learn it!"

She did.

Being a VanDeGrift also meant that she pulled her share of the load at home.

There was the garden to tend to, mowing, or splitting firewood. During the summer she worked alongside the guys, sealing blacktop for the family business on those scorching, endless, shirt-soaking humid days.

Dana was involved in sports, just not to the degree of her siblings. She played soccer, and her father always came to her games. She also ran track one year for him; one year was enough.

She was a good softball player, talented enough to play at Lee College after graduation until a broken collarbone got in the way.

Dana had another side, though, that came from the genteel side of the gene pool. In that way, she was more like her mom. And she did not announce her presence with the unmistakable commanding bullhorn voice of her father or brother. It was softer, like her mother's.

Of that, Jami, says, "She is probably the best of us."

Dana was heavily involved in the arts – theater and drama. She could sing and had a stage presence that won her the lead in the Lebanon High productions of the Wizard of Oz and Oklahoma.

It had started on a whim when she was four years old.

Rosie had seen in the newspaper that the local La Comedia Dinner Theater in nearby Springboro was having auditions for children to play the parts of the Von Trapp siblings in the Sound of Music.

She asked Jami, then 11 years old, if she would like to try out. Jami was thrilled, and while practicing for the rehearsal, she would belt out Do-Re-Mi while Rosie played piano and 4-year-old Dana sat on the bench and sang along.

When it came time to go to tryouts, Dana pleaded to join them, and Rosie said sure, why not – never dreaming she would soon receive a call from the play organizers saying Dana was chosen for a part. A little bit later, another call came in saying Jami was in the cast too.

Dana was an attendant in the LHS Homecoming Court as a freshman. By her senior year, she was the Homecoming Queen.

After college, Dana's path took her to study abroad for a year at Cambridge and later into the classroom as a teacher – in Florida, then back home. She became a wife and mother, with a deeply developed reservoir of faith and a sense of service.

She would need all of that.

CHAPTER 10: A MINI-MIRACLE

He replied, "What is impossible for people is possible with God." – Luke 18:27 (NLT)

Jim was alive on the morning of June 6, less than 24 hours after the fire. It was a mini-miracle that he had made it through the night when the odds said he almost certainly would not, and that was the straw the family had to grasp.

There were other straws, like the twitch of his hand or a slight stirring to consciousness. Was that just muscle reflex, or was God at work? Maybe it was both.

Ty decided to find out. He wanted to make sure his father was awake, so he told Jim to move his foot. Vandy moved his foot slightly. Then his hand twitched again. Was it a reflex, or was he, as Ty believed, trying to tell them something, even though the drugs designed to sedate and keep him as pain-free as possible?

It wasn't a simple process.

With the tubes and all the other medical machines and devices he was attached to, Vandy couldn't speak, so they found a pen, pad and a clipboard. Ty put the pen in his father's hand, and Vandy scratched out on the paper: "Is my face gone?"

There was that question again.

There was no good answer.

There were more questions.

Glasses?

Keys?

He wanted to know what happened to them.

He scribbled a question about whether some checks were deposited in the bank. Can we afford to pay for this?

They told him not to worry.

Can I see?

Will I make it?

Yes, he was assured, through choked breath. You will make it. What else were they going to say? Even in this extremely critical condition, though, Vandy was used to dealing in reality, so he scribbled, "Who says?"

It may have seemed like that was a question without an answer, but the truth is it was already decided. Jim's recovery from the brink would be the story of the journey as much as it was the outcome.

But challenges are just life events that have not yet been conquered. True, doctors weren't giving them much hope, and this wasn't a situation that could be willed away, but there had to be a path to the outcome for which they all prayed. It also was a process, and Ty needed information. He didn't like what he was hearing.

Jim was going to need surgery to remove some damaged tissue, and while explaining this, one of the doctors told Ty that they were going to amputate Jim's left arm. Ty's pulse quickened, and he snapped "absolutely not" back the doctor.

Why, if it seemed so medically necessary?

Because it would take away his father's dignity, and at that moment, it seemed that was all he had left.

The medical man was insistent, if somewhat impatient to explain, there was no alternative. The arm was useless and could make a horrible situation worse. It was infected and could spread gangrene to the rest of his body. It had to go, and it was going to happen. If the doctor was looking for an eventual nod and quiet acceptance of his diagnosis, he was talking to the wrong guy.

The exchange grew increasingly hostile, their raised voices beginning to echo down the hospital corridors as Ty demanded to know the absolute reason why this had to be done, beyond the fact that the arm was badly damaged. Just saying they had to do it was not reason enough. Besides, the doctor had already said Jim was going to die. If that was true, what would be the point of amputating his arm?

When the doctor wouldn't bend, Ty got face-to-face, nose-to-nose, and said with finality, "You are not taking off his left hand."

The standoff ended when the doctor finally walked away. The family and friends gathered in the hospital chapel, on their knees in prayer as Jim prepared for surgery.

They did something else, too. Rosie asked the doctor if it would be okay if they all laid hands on him in prayer, and he agreed. Nephew Bruce Paulus retrieved the key to unlock the chapel, and dozens of people quickly assembled for praise, prayer, and worship. Did that have anything to do with what happened next? The faithful would say it did because Jim' blood pressure dropped dangerously low -- far too low to operate.

That was another moment spent in the valley, a frightful and helpless time for everyone as the inevitable seemed one step closer. Things happen for a reason, though, and the people on their knees in the chapel may have seen their prayers answered in a way that was hard to comprehend in the heat of the moment. Had his blood pressure crashed during surgery, it could have killed him. Instead, doctors decided to let him be – left arm and all – and assumed he would soon be dead.

There was more trauma and prayer, including a neighborhood vigil from six families back in Lebanon back who were close neighbors of the VanDeGrifts, when the surgery finally was performed.

"God was surely with Jim and the doctors," Rosie wrote. "The doctors told us they nearly lost him. Many family members were here, and after surgery, we all went to the chapel to pray. We all spent the night at the hospital with very little sleep."

The family was groggy and numb, but Jim was still here when, by almost any measuring, he shouldn't have been. The sun kept rising and setting, and he was still with them – one day, one heartbeat, at a time.

CHAPTER 11: ACCEPTANCE

Trust in the Lord with all
your heart; do not depend
on your own understanding.
– Proverbs 3:5 (NLT)

Jim was alive and was beating the odds, but he wasn't in the clear. Infection is the constant fear for burn victims, and he was having increasing problems with that. There were other issues, too. Even though his condition had stabilized, the brief bout with consciousness that led to his scribbled questions had given way to unresponsiveness. It seemed to be lasting too long.

"Doctor is concerned," Rosie wrote. "Had CAT scan. Sees no damage."

Just because they didn't see brain damage, doctors told her that mean it wasn't there. Doctors agreed with Rosie it was a big concern, although it might not show for weeks, maybe longer, its effects impossible to predict. It had been such an emotional time, exhausting and draining – struggling to eat, or sleep, or do anything but hang upon the next sliver of news, trying to read voice tones and facial expressions for doctors who had seen it all before. The mention of brain damage seemed to make the valley hills insurmountably steep, and Rosie was in a place of the lost, not knowing what to do.

She asked Bill Cain how she should pray in this situation because she didn't know. Little could she know that this was a defining crossroad of her life.

Until that moment, she had prayed only that her husband is healed. But brain damage? It was a stabbing, knee-buckling thought. What kind of life would this vibrant and fiercely independent man have if he was forced to depend on others for necessities, denied the life he had embraced for all his years?

Would he even know her, or his children and grandchildren? Would he ever be able to experience the something he had taken for granted for so many years? Could he play another round of golf or enjoy an autumn night of Lebanon High football? Would he ever enjoy the powerful music of the marching band, the beauty of a game he loved, or even the way a chilling breeze in the early evening air could make everyone feel alive?

Some things are worse than death. It was all about trust.

That was on their minds as Rosie, Ty, Jami, and Dana stood together in the ICU, just the four of them, clasping hands in prayer. Ty began to hum the tune to "How Great Thou Art." Jami began to sing the words. Everyone joined in.

People talk about turning matters over to God, but at that moment, Rosie learned what that meant. Even in the shadow of death, she sensed there was a lighted path to surrender.

If the God she had worshiped her entire life would welcome her husband into a glorious eternity instead of keeping him prisoner in a failing body, how could she plead for him to stay? No, that would be awful. That would be wrong. That would be putting her grief ahead of her husband's well-being, and that meant releasing everything to God.

Was the Spirit speaking to her at that moment? Probably. Jim had often talked about his relationship with Jesus Christ, and Rosie has that too. The fire had magnified everything, though. This was as real and personal as it gets. So, through her sobs and pain that seared her soul, she chose conscious concession and choked out the words, "Thy will be done."

She meant it.

Not long after, around 4 or maybe 5 p.m., she remembers looking through one of the hospital windows and seeing a spectacular rainbow outside, arching over the sun. Did she see something through her tears? Was it a sign that her prayer had been heard? Maybe, because no one else remembers seeing the rainbow. Maybe it was just for her.

What she does know is that an indescribable feeling came over her, a feeling that Jesus was in the room and had wrapped them all in his arms.

Her husband might live.

He might die.

But she was living with the peace that passes all understanding for eternity, the freedom that comes with surrender. God was in control, and He would never abandon them

That feeling spread throughout the family.

Dana also came to understand that surrender could mean letting her father go. Let him go? After she had prayed so hard for his healing?

Yes, she had to trust that God would know what was best. That's how she could say, "If You need to take my father, so he doesn't suffer, your will be done."

Getting to that point was a spiritual journey through a deep valley filled with fears, known and unknown, that can crop up from unguarded entrances. Hours can seem like days waiting in the emergency room for news. Your mind puts up so many defenses. Not only that, it's exhausting – physically and +mentally. Fear saps your strength and leaves you spent from dealing with uncertainty about the future, and maybe some suppressed anger.

Mostly, it's helplessness. That can be the most draining thing of all. The helplessness caught up with Dana in one moment. She was the only one of the siblings who wasn't married. Pleading, she told her father he couldn't die because he hadn't walked her down the aisle.

People sometimes say God is never closer than when He seems farthest away. Dana would come to realize just how close when she went to the hospital chapel to pray while her dad was having surgery a few days after the fire.

Later she found out his heart had stopped during the operation. She thinks about that time even now, years later. Why did he survive the fire when so many others did not survive similar accidents?

She answers hesitantly.

"I think we need to see God's power over life and death," she said. "I could feel that. I remember feeling that peace that transcends everything, that passes all understanding. An unnatural calm came over me. We wanted him to live, definitely, but we surrendered because we knew he was suffering. Only God knows what's best."

Kelly Pickworth, one of Vandy's former football players, remembered talking with Ty on the phone shortly after the accident. He asked his friend how he was doing, and Ty's answer surprised him:

"Little Pick, I'm doing OK."

Pickworth was instantly puzzled. How could Ty say that he was doing OK? His father probably going to die and he was doing OK? How could that be?

"Things like this happen," Ty said quietly. "When they do, you find out who you belong to."

Those words almost knocked the breath out of Pickworth, and he fought to find something to say in response. All that came out was, "Tiger, you're in the fire now."

"Yeah," Ty said, "but no matter what happens to Dad, it's going to be OK."

Pickworth understood, and decades later, that conversation still resonates with him.

"The legacy of Jim VanDeGrift is seen in his family," he said. "When you raise a son and two daughters who can face something like this the way they did, you see what the man at home and his sweet wife planted in them. The thing he passed to his family was to trust in God Almighty."

It would be OK, either way, because there is liberation in surrender. And hours passed, and the sun continued to rise and set, the man who was supposed to be dead passed milestone after milestone.

The grotesque swelling of his head had begun to subside as well, and his vital signs were stable. Family members were taking turns spending the night at the hospital, and friends brought food and gave them a chance to take a break.

And there was this: "Respirator off. One week (Praise God!). Breathing on his own. Not very responsive, but doctors are OK with that."

There was also a guardian angel at the hospital.

Vicky Barnthouse was a freshman cheerleader when Vandy came to Lebanon. Her brother, Gary Lee, was an outstanding athlete and eventually played quarterback for Vandy. Vicky became a nurse and manager at Miami Valley Hospital.

She had gotten to know him well in high school. He was her driver's education instructor, and one day he had the students drive the 25 miles or so to Wilmington, where the Cincinnati Bengals of the National Football League were holding summer drills.

A man in a brown suit and hat struck up a conversation with her on the sidelines as they watched practice. Did she like football? Tell me about yourself. The man was friendly and kind.

Vandy later asked if she knew who she had been speaking with, but she did not.

It was the legendary founder of the Bengals, Paul Brown.

Vandy never let her live that down.

She was on duty the day of the fire and quickly learned that the man she used to call Mr. VanDeGrift was on his way and in a desperate fight for his life. He would be her patient.

Seeing patients in life-threatening straits was an everyday event in her job. She had learned to tell which ones could beat the odds, and there was one thing about this situation that she strongly believed. No matter what logic said, the man she had come to know and admire was going to make it.

"I have never seen a family so united by one goal – to get him out of that hospital," she said. "This really wasn't a struggle for me. Ultimately, in all my years as a nurse, I learned that no one decides whether they're going to live or die. It's God.

"But if anyone was going to make a miracle happen, it was Jim. He is such a special human being. He almost wills things to happen, and they do."

There was a lot of will at work at that hospital, and everyone involved will tell you it was divinely sent. And so it was that eight days after the accident, Jim opened his eyes for the first time. Another miracle. Two days later, Rosie wrote this entry into her journal:

"Jim had a restful and stable night. HAPPY FATHER'S DAY!"

It was happier than she even knew.

Back in Lebanon on that Sunday morning, Ty went to the front of the Presbyterian Church with something to say. The pews were filled that day as fathers celebrated the day with their families. The normal thing would have been to acknowledge all the dads in the house, preach the sermon, and watch the stampede to Frisch's, a regional restaurant chain famous for Big Boy hamburgers, or someplace else to beat the crowd for lunch with the family.

Not this time, though.

Everyone in the church knew Ty. Many of them had watched him grow from a boy, to a quarterback, and into the principled man who stood before them. Most of them had been on their knees since the fire, and Ty came to offer a message of thanks from the family for the prayers, visits, and general acts of kindness the people had shown. He shared a message of praise, faith, hope, and trust in the healing power of God.

Everybody knew what Ty was saying.

The way pastor Bill Cain remembers it, this was the time to break with business as usual for Presbyterians. While the faith of people in that church can run deeply, they aren't overly demonstrative. Still, Cain felt the nudge from his soul to make an altar call.

"It just seemed like the right time to invite anyone who hadn't surrendered their life to Jesus Christ to come forward and do so, or for anyone else who just wanted to come up and pray," he said.

Ty was the first to kneel, clasping his hands in supplication and thanks. Someone joined him. Then others. More and more. Pretty soon, the front of the church filled with people kneeling to offer thanks and gratitude, along with maybe some who for the first time realized God is real – in good times, and especially in times like this.

What better time for that than Father's Day?

Cain noticed something else, too.

Many of those coming forward were men, strong and stoic, some with tears in their eyes. What was happening here?

Everyone was only beginning to find out.

CHAPTER 12: THE BLOOD DRIVE

Let us think of ways to motivate one another to acts of love and good works. – Hebrews 10:24 (NLT)

Jim's injuries were big news throughout the Miami Valley. The hometown Lebanon newspaper, the Western Star, printed a large graphic of the high school's Warriors logo on the front page with a teardrop sliding down the cheek. It also was news that Lebanon was organizing a blood drive on Vandy's behalf, and a local television reporter wanted to talk with Rosie about that.

She wrote: "I really didn't want to do it, but (the reporter) was doing it for the blood drive and since that will help so many others as well as Jim, I went ahead and did it."

Along with LHS principal Sam Isom, Earl Daniel, a maintenance worker at the high school, was one of the organizers. Like so many, he was paying forward kindness the coach had shown him.

He got to know Jim while a volunteer around the football program. They hit it off immediately. After graduation, Daniel was laid off from work. Vandy jumped in. He told Daniel to go back home, put on some nice clothes, and to see the superintendent.

There was a job waiting for him.

They worked with the blood bank in Dayton. So many people were asking how they could help, and a blood drive was the perfect solution. While they were setting it up, officials at the blood bank asked how many donors they were expecting.

Earl guessed it would be about a hundred. They had heard that number many times at the blood bank for other drives. Everyone always estimates a hundred. The usual turnout is about 10, but this was not your usual blood drive.

It was scheduled for Sunday, June 22 – about two and a half weeks after the fire – at the high school cafeteria. It was supposed to run from 1-5 p.m., but by 11 a.m. there was already a line of donors waiting. A blood bank worker saw the line and got on the phone immediately. Send help! We don't have enough people here!

The line kept growing until it snaked outside the cafeteria as people waited their turn. Ty and Jami spoke to people at the drive; it was their first time out in public since the accident.

People donated 150 pints of blood that day, and that number would have been far greater, but the bank ran out of materials to draw and store the blood. To Earl, it looked like at least another hundred people in line had to be turned away. Some of those people left in tears.

Do you ever hear of a blood drive where organizers had to stop accepting donors? It doesn't happen often, but it did that day in Lebanon.

Back at the hospital, Vandy was sitting up in a chair at times, sometimes for more than an hour. The swelling was going down, and nurses became convinced that they saw something that couldn't be fully explained by science. He was off the respirator. His eyes, those unforgettable pools of blue that Rosie noticed that first night when he asked her dance back in Frenchtown, started to look normal. His voice was still a raspy whisper, but nurses could understand him when he barked, "Stop that" as they tried to tend to him.

That voice. Those eyes. That drive and inner will. It was all there.

The burns that seemed certain to kill him were beginning to heal. And by June 24, only 19 days after flames engulfed him, Jim transferred from ICU to the hospital specialized burn unit.

"I remember Jami and I were at the hospital, and we were looking out the window, and these big storm clouds were rolling in," Dana said. "I looked at Jami, and she said, 'The same God that is controlling these clouds is healing Dad.'"

Yes, this was a miracle happening -- perhaps from the power of prayer, or maybe the result of modern medicine and superior hospital care.

Who says it couldn't be both?

Miracles aren't restricted to human scheduling, though. Yes, Vandy's recovery had divine fingerprints all over it, but in some ways, the hard part was beginning. There were many miles to go, and everyone involved still needed each other.

Burn victims endure a tedious and excruciating procedure known as debridement, where dead skin is removed so new, healthy skin has a chance to grow. Dead skin increases the risk of potentially fatal infection.

For Jim, that meant enduring hour-long sessions two or three times a day while nurses picked at the decaying burned flesh with tweezers. It's not as simple as it sounds. Removing the old skin can aggravate the nerve endings of healthy skin in the affected area, and that can be agonizing.

Bleeding also is an unavoidable part of the procedure, and that meant changing his dressings several times a day. Until new skin was applied, his exposed arms looked like someone had dipped them in bright red paint from his wrist to his shoulder.

That was more agony, and that wasn't even the worst of it.

Because of the burns, scar tissue covered large portions of his body. Left unchecked it would slowly encase Jim in an unyielding shell. To limit that as much as possible, therapists worked hours with Jim daily, stretching his skin to give him more range of motion.

Doctors removed healthy skin from his right hip, right calf, and his high groin area to replace destroyed tissue on his face and arms. They cultured and grew more than 200 pieces of his skin in strips that measured 1-by-1 inch and were then stapled back onto his body. Even under sedation, he awoke in the middle of one procedure. That was not a good moment for anyone.

His injuries became part of a case study for the treatment of burn victims. One of the doctors in the study selected Jim because he never saw a case so severe.

He had a massive blister on his left arm and shoulder. His ear was torched and puffed. He had a huge scar in the shape of a backward "C."

His left arm, the one a doctor wanted to amputate, was already frozen in place like it was in a cast. Stretching it even an inch or two was excruciating, but there was no other choice. Therapists repeated the stretching all over the affected areas of Jim's body, hour after hour.

Even now, his arm has the feel of a large tree root – hard and unyielding.

A special facial mask was also part of the equation. A Lebanon High graduate and a member the Presbyterian church where Jim and Rosie have attended since 1967, Jennifer McKenzie Whitestone, was on the team that designed the mask, which dramatically helped reduce swelling and scaring for victims. Doctors in the past had designed the form-fitting masks through painful clay moldings taken from the face. The new type of mask was designed for the individual face by a laser. Doctors would spread lotion on Vandy's face, then set the mask. It helped smooth his skin.

But if everyone measured his recovery in heartbeats, sunrises,

and sometimes painful screams, a journey of many miles with untold more to go was taking a toll on Rosie.

She had been so strong throughout the ordeal, but everyone has their limits. Most nights, she slept on a leather sofa outside the room where doctors and nurses kept watch over Jim. Hospital staff provided pillows and blankets and what comfort they could, but some things were unavoidable – such as the night when the family members of another patient got into a violent, scary screaming match that nearly led to punches or worse.

Family and friends remained in constant prayer for Jim, but what about her? Rosie needed them too.

"Rosie was not having a good day," she wrote in her journal.

Ginny Kuntz, who had helped clear the hospital hallways at Rosie's request on the night of the fire, once again became the answer to a prayer that may not have have been spoken out loud but had reached God nonetheless.

Friends got Rosie out of the hospital for dinner at the Pine Club, one of the best steak houses in Dayton. Other friends, like Talitha Colston, made sure she had hot coffee and breakfast in the morning at the hospital.

The big concern was Jim's unresponsiveness. Nurses were increasingly worried about that, and the lead doctor called for another CAT scan and a neurosurgeon.

Can God reach you on a roller-coaster?

Of course.

Consider this entry into Rosie's journal two weeks to the day after the fire.

"Wonderful quiet time with God."

As the song says, be still and know that I am God. It had been so hard to keep still, what with fear keeping a non-ceasing grip on almost every waking moment. It seemed like sudden desperate concerns had spoiled every good moment.

Then there were the sheer logistics. Family schedules were juggled. Friends were stopping by all the time, wanting to bring food or anything else they could. Although everyone had spent so much time in prayer – Rosie, especially – those were desperate cries toward heaven for a miracle. In times like this, Rosie just needed some quiet time alone with God, not so much to talk – there's a pretty good chance God knew what she wanted by that point – but to be held in the divine embrace.

The answer came in the form of another dream by her husband. Unlike the dream he had in the immediate aftermath of the fire, he wasn't chased by the evil he couldn't recognize. This time he was with friends and family at a restaurant. Everyone was happy. Kids were there. He didn't know then what it meant, except that, "It felt glorious."

Dana saw something else, too. God doesn't waste an opportunity.

Remember how she pleaded for her father to live so he could walk her down the aisle?

During the crisis, some friends came to the hospital to give Dana a break and take her out to eat. Included in the group was a guy named Spence Cropper from nearby Centerville.

There is a story behind that.

Dana and Spence had met in childhood. Spence wasn't a Lebanon High man, but something kept drawing him there anyway.

He read about Dana's athletic exploits in the Western Star, the local Lebanon paper. His grandfather had an RV and used to travel to every Lebanon football game, home or away. Spence rode along.

His aunt, Ginny Kuntz, kept nudging him to ask Dana out. He remembers thinking, "She's a pretty cute girl."

That wasn't enough for Ginny. She kept playing matchmaker, but it seemed like Dana was always dating someone else, or he was – it just never worked out.

They almost connected a couple of times, but nothing happened until the accident.

"Ginny calls me and asked if I'd be willing to go up to the hospital and help get Dana out of there for a night," Spence recalled.

Of course, he was.

He was dating someone else at the time, so that girlfriend went with him. He remembers walking around the University of Dayton, trying to take Dana's mind off what was happening. He suggested they should all go to a movie.

For reasons even they can't explain, they chose the action film "Con Air."

There is a scene in the middle of the movie where someone was burned. Everyone in the group walked out of the theater and, well, that's that.

Except it wasn't.

Jim had made it through the worst of it by the fall of October 1997. Spence was working as a CPA by then, ready to go on a date with a young lady in Alabama, when he got a phone call.

Ginny Kuntz and Rosie were still working to make this union happen.

They told him he should call Dana. Maybe see if they could get together.

He wasn't sure about the whole thing, so that's when he was told

– in no uncertain terms – no, call her.

Now.

It wasn't a suggestion.

She is expecting your call.

They got together.

Even in something as awful as this accident, things can work out.

"Spence was with my mom and dad when he asked for permission to marry me," Dana said. "One of the stipulations was that he had to be in church every Sunday."

Not a problem.

And when the big day arrived, and her father prepared to join her on a walk down the aisle in answer to a prayer, Jim leaned over to his youngest daughter and said simply, "I love you."

Doesn't the father always say that to his daughter in such moments?

Yes, mostly.

But Jim rarely expressed such emotions, at least in words. His love showed in how he cared for others more than himself but saying those three words – I love you – was a challenge at times.

"Dad was always big on the idea that every day should be a great day, and that God is good – all the time," Dana said. "He has such a great attitude for life. But before the accident, I don't recall a lot of times when he said I love you. After the accident, he said it a lot."

CHAPTER 13: ROAD TO RECOVERY AND ANOTHER JOLT

And my God will meet all your needs according to the riches of his glory in Christ Jesus. – Philippians 4:19 (NLT)

When it became clear Jim going to live, it was time to think about getting back into the routine the family knew before the fire.

Ty and was preparing to return to Florida, where his wife, Mary, had kept the trains running in the household, paying the bills and such, while he mostly tended to his father. Mary had gone back and forth from Tampa to the hospital a few days while neighbors and friends from their church pitched in with things like yard mowing. Dana had gotten a teaching job near her brother's home and was heading to Florida, too.

Jami and her husband needed to tend to a housing matter in Colorado.

After two months of high stress that had torn at their inner beings, life was returning to a semblance of normal.

The family, particularly Rosie, had seen so much during that hospital stay. She shared with friends her anguish at watching as others would come there needing emergency care, but without the foundational faith that sustained a family and town during the awful days of fear, doubt, and halting recovery.

What must it be like for the living lost?

Prayer, faith, and the support of friends and strangers coming together in the community had sustained the VanDeGrifts during this trial, but they weren't finished.

Doctors applied the last of the skin grafts in early August, and the surgery left Vandy tired and drowsy. He had to wear arm splints, which he didn't like. The parts of his body where healthy skin had to be removed for grafts were painful. That lasted for days.

Dana remembers that doctors used pig skin for some of the temporary grafts on his chest. For an old football coach, that was appropriate.

Therapy was going well, though – with the inevitable competition from the patient. Jim needed calories, which the hospital staff tried to provide. He didn't care much for the menu, though, and so a game of sorts began where Jim would try to flip cookies from his dinner tray into a nearby trash can.

He wasn't always successful, which left a mess for nurses to clean when they came into the room. It was just part of the slow, steady grind toward recovery. There was no way to rush through it.

The slice of normal life granted to the family suddenly went askew. Early on the morning of August 16, on the day Ty and his family were to return to Florida, the family received another jolt.

"The Lord came at 12:20 this morning to take Pop home," Rosie wrote. "Ty and Jami went to Greenville hospital at 10:30 last night to be with family there. I couldn't go; I was too sick. Then they came to the hospital to tell Jim."

Maurice VanDeGrift had died.

That's the father who told Jim to pick up the shovel. His Midwestern sensibility and deep love of family were part of his son's DNA. He was 86 years old.

And the son couldn't go to his father's funeral.

They considered trying to get Jim there in an ambulance, but the risk of infection was still too great. So, Earl Daniel and Bill Fisher – who used to coach with Vandy – went back to the hospital after the funeral and relayed everything about the service.

And later, on the day the funeral, Cain performed a special memorial service in the hospital for Vandy.

"We all stopped by to see him on the way back from Pop's funeral," Rosie wrote. "Jim seemed very sad."

In the middle of preparations for the funeral and saying farewells to those who had to leave after spending two months at his bedside, there was one other important change: Jim moved from the burn center to a rehabilitation room.

He had a lifetime of painful, at times excruciating, physical therapy ahead. It would involve therapists and, later, Rosie, twisting, bending and pushing his arms, shoulders, and legs in thrice-daily sessions designed to break up scar tissue.

Yes, he was going to live.

He had come through the fire.

And God had work for him to do, along with, maybe, a special gift from heaven. A few friends were waiting when the car carrying him home from the hospital pulled into the driveway. And Katie, the family's golden retriever, bounded over and greeted the passenger like only a faithful dog can, wagging her tail in utter joy as her tongue darted toward Jim's face.

Everyone was a little scared that Katie could have knocked her master over with her exuberance, but this wasn't a time to be afraid. Welcome home, the world seemed to shout.

We missed you.

Yes, a miracle had pulled Jim back from the brink of death, and everyone saw it. The story doesn't end there, though. It wouldn't have ended even had he succumbed to the fire.

Jim had started a Fellowship of Christian Athletes chapter not long after he arrived in Lebanon. The FCA was more than a club. It was an extension of the family, which is core to Jim's beliefs. Meetings would start with individual testimony, sharing, and support. They talked about being thankful, having discipline, and living like Jesus.

Steve Pickworth was an incoming freshman when he joined the group and signed up to attend an FCA camp in Greenville, South Carolina, with several other members.

He gave his life to Christ at that camp. When people ask today who led him there, he answers, "My high school football coach."

There is a line that coaches must be aware of when it comes to religion. They are technically employees of the state, and there are laws about keeping religion separate from work. That's especially true in the classroom.

You can preach by the way you live, though, and that's how Vandy operated. He wouldn't push religion on his players, but he never shied from it, either. Players soon learned it wasn't about forcing Bible verses down their throats or checking to make sure they made it to church on Sunday.

It was about living an authentic life of integrity, and anyone curious to know more found out that he gave credit to Jesus. Leading by that example stuck with Steve Pickworth.

"In those FCA meetings, he always told us that the first person in your life should be Jesus Christ," he said. "Even your family has to come second to Jesus."

Joining FCA under Jim was a participation sport. The summer after he arrived in Lebanon, he organized a bicycle trip to Winona Lake, Indiana to hear an up and coming preacher named Billy Graham. The trip was about 175 miles from Lebanon, and about 15 hours of riding time by bicycle along some backroads flanked by miles and miles of cornfields still green and growing, waving in the warm summer breezes.

Six FCA members joined Jim on the venture – Rosie, Ty, and Jami followed in the car, although Jami was dropped off in Arcanum along the way.

There were some breakdowns along the way for malfunctioning bicycle chains, and Jim remembers that "it was against the wind. It seemed like it was uphill all the way."

The riders camped out during the trip, which allowed the kind of lasting fellowship that can only exist under the stars and around a fire. The payoff was that everyone got to within a few yards of Billy Graham, but something else had sparked there. The trips became a regular thing, not all as long as the original one for sure, but long enough to get the message across that something special was happening.

More FCA members began to sign up. Fathers joined their sons and the coaches for day-long bonding. As much as football, FCA became the pebble in the lake that started the larger circle that affected lives over the years.

It wasn't the only way Jim had a lasting impact, though. He likely coached several thousand football players and track athletes over the years, and many of them carry on the traits and values he had instilled through athletics, in the classroom, or just passing them in the school hallway.

Most were from Lebanon, some were from Ansonia, but all share the imprint of the coach's words and example in their lives.

CHAPTER 14: A CHRISTIAN MAN IN THE ARENA

For tremendous power is released through the passionate, heartfelt prayer of a godly believer. – James 5:16 (The Passion Translation)

Time and distance can't erode relationships. Everyone belonged, no matter what.

The circle includes Marty Roe, who was a shy offensive lineman on Vandy's football team but later achieved stardom as the lead singer for the superstar country music band Diamond Rio.

Marty played football and was a miler on the track team. Jim ran a lawn-care service on the side, and it wasn't unusual for him to hire students.

Marty was one of those.

He wasn't big, maybe 150 pounds, but he was the center on the football team. It was a position of increased responsibility. Nothing happened until he snapped the ball.

Marty grew up in a deeply religious family. His father, Zane, was an elder in the Church of Christ for 40 years. There was church on Sunday morning, Sunday night, and Wednesday night – without fail.

It was expected.

Church life can be a sheltered existence, though. Not everyone in the world behaves the way church-going people do. Faith can be a touchy subject in everyday life.

In his head football coach, though, young Marty Roe saw a man who lived his faith. Sure, his father was authentic about spiritual matters, but that's in the house.

"Coach represented something else," Marty said. "Dad didn't follow sports. In that arena, the coach represented what it means to be a Christian man."

A tradition for seniors under Vandy was to have their pastor deliver a message and prayer to the team before a game or at some other time. That wasn't going to be a problem for someone like Marty, but what about the other players? Maybe some of them didn't go to church. There is no suggestion that the coach embarrassed anyone who couldn't come up with a spiritual leader, but there's another side to this.

In Lebanon, Ohio, the head football coach was a towering figure in those days. If players didn't attend church and had to scramble to find someone to fill the coach's request, most of them did.

"For some of them, that might have been their first exposure to a Christian man other than their coach," Marty said.

Growing up in the church had another advantage for young Marty Roe. It gave him a chance to sing and play guitar in public, and his football coach taught him the importance of accepting responsibility and leadership.

Those worlds combined when he became the lead singer and rhythm guitar player for Diamond Rio, a country and Christian band. Their first single – "Meet In the Middle" – spent two weeks atop the Billboard Hot Country Songs. That was the first time any debut country single had climbed that high.

The band has three platinum albums, 13 Grammy nominations, and two top vocal group awards from the Academy of Country Music. By 1997, they were spending 225 nights a year touring at stops all over the country. That got interrupted, though, when

Marty Roe heard about the fire that threatened the life of the man he had grown so much to admire.

He told Rosie he'd like to come to visit.

"Well, he's pretty drugged up and out of it."

"I'm coming anyway."

Marty and his dad met Rosie outside Jim's hospital room. He wasn't sure Vandy would even be awake, but he was surprised when the coach greeted him with a raspy, "Marty Roe!" as he walked through the door.

Marty joined hands with his father, Rosie, and Dana, and they prayed. And at that moment, everything crystallized. He loved Vandy, but he didn't fully grasp all the lessons he had learned both on and off the football field.

Marty had wanted most to be a jock while in high school. He didn't let a lot of people outside his church know how well he could sing. Vandy had taught him to attack life, though, and singing was in his heart.

Vandy has no memory of that day when Marty came to visit. Almost a year later, though, they met again. Vandy does remember that one.

It was the first anniversary of the fire, and it was time to finish the golf game that never got to happen the year before.

On a wet, windy afternoon, Marty, his father, and Ty joined Jim on the first tee, and they played 18 holes. There were only a few people on the course that day, so there was no rush. Rain pelted throughout much of the round, but Vandy couldn't feel the drops because there were no nerve endings on the skin covering his arms.

No matter.

They weren't dealing with pain on the anniversary of Vandy's death. No sir.

"Bonus time," Vandy called it.

This was a celebration of life.

CHAPTER 15: A VOICE FROM THE PAST

Love empowers us to fulfill the law of the Anointed One as we carry each other's troubles.
– Galatians 6:2 (TPT)

Celebrating life means sharing the blessing.

Jim always did that, of course, and he never forgot where he came from. Lebanon is not the only place where the lessons Jim taught still echo through the decades, and the three seasons he spent as head coach at Unioto High School before coming to Lebanon will always be part of who he is.

That's why he didn't hesitate after receiving a phone call that Lloyd Davis, who played for Jim at Unioto, was in a hospital battling Stage 4 cancer. He hadn't kept in touch with Davis, but upon hearing the news of his condition time and distance melted.

Some people might have sent a card. Others might have called the hospital to offer a word of encouragement.

Jim? He drove the hour and 15 minutes from Lebanon to Chillicothe to visit a player he hadn't seen in untold years. He went to offer comfort and support, and Davis recognized his coach immediately.

Mike Juenger also played for Jim at Unioto, a center and middle linebacker for the Shermans. Mike loved everything about football, and he was thrilled when the new coach drilled the team on fundamentals, over and over again until they got it right. In Vandy, he had found a coach whose passion for the game was on par with his own.

And there was that voice – that powerful, commanding, in-charge voice that made high school boys believe they could do anything their coach de-manded. That voice scared Mike to his marrow, but only with the fear that comes from letting down someone he deeply admired. He found that out with emphasis during a scrimmage game. A player on the other team had delivered three hard blows upside his head, and Mike was losing his cool.

"What's wrong?" Vandy barked at him.

"That son of a bitch hit me in the mouth."

What happened next was old-school coaching. Vandy grabbed Mike's facemask and spun him around like a helicopter, or-dering him to the bench in humiliation as the other players cowered and wondered what he had done to deserve that. Vandy wasn't mad because of the way Mike was playing, though. It was something much more.

You don't cuss on Vandy's football team.

"I don't want ever to hear you use that kind of language again!"

Mike needed those kinds of lessons, though. He needed more than a football coach in his life. His parents had divorced, leaving his mother to raise him and his brother. The coach with the bullhorn voice and strict ways of behaving filled in some missing gaps in ways only a strong male authority figure could at the time.

There was something else about this coach, though – a vulnerability of sorts. He had been around sports all his life and had never seen a man cry until he met this football coach. Not even his father.

It usually happened before a game, when the coach would walk among his players as they went through warmups. They had spent all week preparing for battle, and the time was at hand. He wanted them to feel the passion, dedication, and, yes, love he had for them.

They could count on more of the same in those moments before he sent them out of the locker room and into whatever awaited on the field. It wasn't a ploy. His voice would reach deep inside his boys, rising with honest emotion about the work they had done and the challenge they faced.

And then it would happen. The intensity of the moment was often overwhelming. Jim's words would become more choked and earnest, and this rugged, larger-than-life man wasn't ashamed when his players saw the moisture trickle down the sides of his cheeks. He wanted them to know how much he cared, and every one of them had better care at least that much too.

They did, of course.

Unioto's players answered his challenge by going 17-0-1 in his final two seasons as coach.

High school is a short time in everyone's lives, but it seems to last forever. After life had thrown its share of punches at him, Mike Juenger came back to the father-coach from Unioto he had learned to love, trust and believe.

It had been 10 or 15 years since he and Coach had talked, time enough for Mike to have gone through a divorce, a stint in the military, a couple of job changes, a move to Texas, a second marriage, and a transfer to England.

He was successful at his job in international sales, but it was a demanding job, and the pressure to excel in business was causing more problems at home. Those lessons from long ago kept coming back, though. His old high school coach had taught him about being a man, and maybe he would do that again.

Mike picked up the phone and dialed area code 5-1-3.

By the time he hung up, Jim knew his former player was in trouble. And Juenger knew his former coach wanted to help. He didn't know how much until a few years later after he moved to Cleveland and was in a hospital bed recovering from open heart surgery.

The phone rang in the room.

"Hello?"

"How are you doing?"

The voice jumped out of the phone, and Mike recognized it immediately. It was like he was back in school again. They talked for an hour, but happily ever after often works on its own schedule. They promised to keep in touch, and they did, but true change comes from the inside, and that can take some time – in this case, after ten years, and more potholes in his life.

Mike was back in the hospital for his second heart surgery, thinking about his own mortality, when he remembered something else about Coach – something besides the demands, the life lessons, the voice from which no one could hide, and those tears that flowed without embarrassment before a football game.

He remembered hearing his coach pray out loud to the team in the locker room.

The words came flowing back, that powerful man authentically humbling himself with those earnest requests to a God he seemed to understand is real. Keep players safe, Lord. Help us give our best. We give you the glory, our Father in heaven.

Those words planted a seed inside of Mike that he was only now beginning to understand finally. The coach wasn't just repeating some words to get his players in the proper mood for the game was moments away. It was much more than that. He was sharing a heartfelt belief in something larger than us all. But through all the years that followed, Mike still wondered: who is the God that his coach knew so well?

He had to find out.

He went to church sometimes and even had mouthed the words of acceptance of Christ into his life, but how could he be sure he was doing it right? Why was everything so confusing? Why did he keep messing up? There had to be something deeper, but those answers come when and how they will.

Overflowing with need, he dialed 5-1-3 again.

It was at 2 a.m.

He talked. Coach listened.

They talked about the Bible and the guidance within its pages.

You don't have to be an expert in Holy Scriptures, Coach told him. It's more important to be faithful than it is to be a scholar. God will take it from there.

Vandy shared his morning routine. When the house was quiet, and his mind was fresh, he would listen to a Bible on the compact disc while having his coffee. He would listen some more while driving his truck to chores when it was just him and God, and he could roll up the windows to block out the world.

Sometimes he listened for five minutes.

Sometimes he listened for an hour.

The Bible. Yeah, that's where to begin the search for answers that had thus far been elusive.

On the other end of the telephone, Mike Juenger had one of those life-changing moments. He decided then and there he would get serious about giving life to beliefs he had kept largely submerged inside a life lacking in true purpose. His goal: Read all 66 books of the Bible in one year.

He finished in 10 months.

Don't get it twisted. No one gets peace by completing a reading project to prove they can. For Mike, that peace and a hunger to know much more came from following through on a meaningful commitment he promised to do. It wasn't a task; it was the beginning of a deep, lasting relationship with a living God whose arms are ever-outreaching, waiting for Mike to be willing to be held in his embrace.

He has thought about the twists of life from time to time that brought about this change. He thought about the coach from long ago who had become a lifelong friend, and how being available when the phone rings – even if it's 2 a.m. – is a powerful and effective witness for the Spirit that lived inside the man.

"The things he said then stuck with me. I took it to heart," Mike said. "Every time I thought about it, it would always come back to those conversations I had with Coach. That's what made the difference."

CHAPTER 16: THE GIFT OF TIME

He told them, "My soul is crushed with grief to the point of death. Stay here and keep watch with me." – Matthew 26:38 (NLT)

Jeff Norris played wide receiver and defensive back for the Warriors. He was a good player, and like most of those who played in the VanDeGrift era, he saw a complex but honest man at work.

"To me, he coached at the moment," Norris said. "He was intimidating when he needed to be and comforting when it was called for."

And during Norris' senior year, it was called for after his grandmother died.

"I was very close to her, and I was crying when I went in to see Coach Van DeGrift," he said. "He asked me one question – was she a Christian? I said, yes, she was. And he said, "I know you'll miss her, but there's nothing to worry about.

"And he was right. I'll see her again. It really calmed me down. I've carried that with me ever since."

That's just one story out of many lives that were affected by the coach. Most of them aren't famous. They have names like Mike Bain, Jim Norris, Tim Caan, Brad Nixon, Tim Bashford, Todd Toliver, Don Juszczyk – nicknamed "Juice" because Vandy couldn't pronounce his last name.

Juice was an undersized and not-very-athletic sophomore who wasn't going to get much playing time for a team coming off an appearance in the state championship game. On a lot of teams, he would have been practice fodder for the better players.

But he was a Warrior, and as Vandy told him pointedly during one practice, "You are part of Warrior football. You are here to play football."

He got some field time during a blowout win against Mason midway through the season, playing linebacker as the opponents drove to the 23-yard-line late in the game. Juice misread a coverage on a play and missed the chance at an interception and possible touchdown.

No big deal, he thought. I'm just a sophomore nobody.

But he wasn't a nobody. He was a Warrior; a point emphasized when Vandy ran the play back multiple times during film study the next day. Each time, Juice saw the missed opportunity. Vandy was in his ear the whole time, to reinforce the point.

He never forgot it.

He's grown up now with all the responsibilities of adulthood, but that blown coverage is always there. When he comes home to Lebanon for holidays, he makes a point to go to the 23-yard line and reflect – not about the mistake so much, but about the lesson of being prepared and doing things right every time.

"I still hear that voice of Coach VanDeGrift telling me I'm a winner, don't quit, walk it like you talk it, and remember your morals," he said. "He taught me pride and self-worth. He was the biggest mentor in my life, whether he knew it or not. He made sure we were all part of it. He gave me something. He showed me I belong."

He showed Juice something else, too.

His brother, Pete, was in the hospital after a bad bicycle accident when Vandy came to visit. There were several people in the room when they heard the coach's voice as he walked through the door.

"Hey guys, how are you?"

They told him the truth. You have to tell Vandy the truth. They were all hurting for Pete.

"Let's pray."

They held hands, and Coach asked for healing and relief from pain. After he left, one of the guys asked, "Is it just me? I was hurting before he got here and now I'm not."

The words come tumbling out rapidly now as Juice tries to explain a moment he will never forget.

"That's the aura of Jim VanDeGrift," he said. "No matter where we are, we talk about that time he came to visit. When he's around you, and you hear his voice, something inside you just gets going. You feel his power. That's why I say I learned more about life from him than I did football. When you're in the presence of the man, you know it. I can close my eyes now and hear the locker room door close, and know he was in there. There was a sense of power when he was in the room."

There was a sense of purpose when left, too. Juice is now a doctor.

Consider Todd Toliver, who never played football and says he wasn't much of an athlete. He was having trouble fitting in at high school until Vandy stopped him one day in the hallway and asked out of the blue if he wanted to be a trainer on the football team.

Why did he do that?

Who knows?

"He has something where he can see inside a person and know

what they can be," Toliver said. "I hadn't thought about doing anything like that, but it got me interested."

After high school, he became a hospital orderly, a paramedic, and that eventually led to a supervisor's role at Lebanon's 9-1-1 dispatch. Toliver took the call about a fiery accident with a tractor on that June afternoon in 1997, never dreaming he was sending a rescue squad to help save the life of a man he admired for picking him out in a hallway.

"When I found out who it was, I cried my eyes out," he said. "He was always so encouraging to me. He wanted you to be around. And he helped me so much in my walk of faith. The part of him that is so deep in Christ resonated with me. I learned two big lessons from him: unconditional love and time. Give people your time."

Vandy did that with a track athlete named Tim Caan.

In high school, Tim ran track for four years but will be the first to tell you he wasn't much of a contributor. It took him until his senior year to earn his varsity letter; all seniors got one. He had to juggle classes with his work schedule pumping gas or later at a local tile company.

His hair was long, reaching past his neck and onto his back. He liked to smoke a little pot, drink some beer. College wasn't going to be an option. He didn't know it at the time, but Jim was working behind the scenes on his behalf.

He was in the middle of a class when, he says, "Coach V. literally dragged me out to take a military test." It was an aptitude test to determine which branch of the service recruits are best equipped to enter.

Graduation had passed, and summer had arrived. Cann figured he was finished with LHS, but Vandy wasn't finished with him. He hadn't completed the final portion of his driver's education class, and Vandy didn't like to leave things undone even though the student had graduated.

"He actually hunted me down and made me finish that class," Cann said. "It was just a half-credit, and I didn't need it to graduate, but he told me I had paid for the class and I was going to finish. And then he told me I was going to get a visit that Thursday night at 7:30, and to make sure I was home. I figured it would be Coach V, dropping by for some reason."

It wasn't.

When Cann answered the knock on his door, he saw a Marine staff sergeant. Soon, Tim Cann was a U.S. Marines recruit, headed to boot camp in San Diego. The only people who knew were Cann, the recruiter, and Jim. He only told his mother and family about two weeks before he was scheduled to report.

"I figured if I had survived track with that man, I could survive anything," Cann said. "He wasn't easy on us; he never was. Looking back, I wasn't a star football player. I wasn't a star track athlete. I was just a kid, nothing special. But he cared, and that made all the difference.

"The way I was headed, I probably would have wound up in jail. He helped me get on the right path. He helped a lot of people."

Upon his arrival at basic training, Cann joined other recruits at a quarter-mile track. They dressed in shorts, t-shirts, and boots. The drill instructors told the recruits to run until they couldn't any longer.

The laps flew by.

Quarter-mile.

Half-mile.

Mile.

Some began to drop out. Tim Cann kept running.

He passed a mile and a half.

Two miles.

More dropped out.

Cann made it 16 times around the track in those boots, four miles. He remembers one of the instructors saying, "Looks like we've got a runner" as he went past. And Cann heard another voice as well. It belonged to his track coach at Lebanon High, barking at him to keep moving.

"I was pretty darn thankful right then that I had Jim VanDeGrift as my coach," he said.

He did his four years in the Marines, got married, and raised a family. He kept his hair short and stayed far away from trouble. He never saw Vandy again until one night about 30 years after his high school graduation.

It was a big night of celebration in town. A new high school was about to open, with a large new gymnasium. They wanted to give a fitting goodbye to the old gym, the scene of many triumphs and championships, and a lot of the former players came back to celebrate the memories.

Cann got into a long line waiting to say hello to Vandy. The scars on the coach's face and arms were a jolting sight, but Cann was about to receive a bigger surprise.

He was all set to re-introduce himself to the coach; after all, it had been 30 years. He didn't have long hair anymore, for one thing. And a lot had happened since that raw young boy from Lebanon left to become a Marine.

But not so much that Vandy didn't stick out his hand and call him by name.

"He recognized me instantly," Cann said. "Thirty years. I looked totally different. But he knew me. You think about all the lives that have been affected by that man. Why would he remember me? Why would he care?"

Because he does.

Giving the gift of time took the coach occasionally out of his comfort zone. During a trip to Florida, he was visiting with Tim Borland, another Unioto graduate. Borland was deeply involved in ministry to homeless people and asked Vandy to join him on a visit to one of Tampa's poorest neighborhoods.

Vandy went, of course, into an area north of Ybor City known for crime and drugs, and oh my goodness! It's a long way from the colonial beauty of Lebanon, but God is everywhere, including the narrow back alleys and tiny houses with broken windows in a neighborhood that love seems to have skipped.

While modern skyscrapers glitter as a backdrop to the scene, and expensive condominiums and upscale restaurants are close by, people here live a different existence. Dinner might come from a dumpster. The guy on the street corner at night might be selling death in a bag, and you never know who might be willing to settle a fight with a gun.

But love is powerful, and it was in motion that day because someone took the time to care about those forgotten by others. As Borland and the coach walked through that tough, wary neighborhood, Jim saw the eager way those who have so little material worth rushed forward, shouting hellos, arms extended to embrace the minister who cared for them.

All it took was a little time and a willing heart. And it reinforced the lesson Jim had taught Brad Nixon and so many others: People are always watching.

Nixon was there at the start, an undersized offensive guard on Vandy's first two Lebanon teams. He lives in Los Angeles now, where a quest to reconnect with his old coach led to a phone call and a surprising discovery. Vandy remembered him.

Let's see, Brad Nixon, not very big – 5-foot-9, 135 pounds, fast off the ball but not good foot speed, and very smart.

More than 45 years after he had played his final football game, Brad Nixon heard an accurate scouting report on himself from a straight-talking coach.

"That was so impressive," he said. "I remember Vandy the coach on the field – strong, impressive, all emotion. But he was also a total professional. He was very pragmatic about who we were. He said the same thing about each senior at the senior banquet. He was just honest. And here all these years later, he could rattle it off to me.

"It was a lesson in humility that what distinguished me was that I was smart. It was also a lesson that people are always watching you and evaluating you."

Tim Bashford believed when he played that all that work by the players was to be ready for the next game. He didn't know it got him ready for life.

He holds a management position in a buying cooperative for consumer electronics, where he uses the lessons of effort and preparation that he first learned on the practice field.

You have to be all over the details. You must follow up, follow through, and execute. You must be all in. There must be great expectations.

Success is when preparation meets opportunity.

"It was about the system," Bashford said. "Ultimately, that's it. Everything connects at one point. I hear Coach VanDeGrift tell me that every day."

Many of his former players talk about how seeing their coach's authentic faith affects them, even the ones who aren't believers. It was impossible to see how Vandy lived and not believe a greater force wasn't driving things.

Take the pregame ritual, for instance.

Vandy could summon cinder-block splitting oratory with the best of them, usually accompanied by a cracking voice and a tear-stained face that left his young charges breathing fire and ready to run through a stone wall if that's what it took.

As Jim Norris, one of his former players and coaches put it, "There is an unspoken bond for those who had the privilege of being in Jim's locker room to hear those speeches. Those were unusual moments for a young person to be part of, to get the edge something like that provided."

But those words of power and might – GO GET 'EM! – were always accompanied by prayer, often silent prayer.

Take a knee, men.

The players would all comply.

Bow your heads.

The silence in the room drowned out the echoes from whatever the marching band was playing a hundred yards away on the field in the moments before the team would emerge, ready to go. The young Warriors asked in their ways for intercession in what was about to happen on the field, and maybe some last-minute reassurance from a higher power. But what was their head coach asking for in words none of them could hear?

He was asking God to keep his boys safe.

That's it.

Praying for victory would have been inappropriate. Jim would never ask God to choose sides in Lebanon vs. Edgewood or any other team. Just bring the boys safely through the battle.

Amen.

Getting them ready for battle was the coaches' job, and you didn't get a pass just because you weren't on the first string and not likely to play much in that week's game.

Or in the extraordinary case of a person who realized he wasn't cut out for football, you don't even suit up.

CHAPTER 17: YOU'RE GOING TO QUIT, AREN'T YOU?

Don't you realize that in a race everyone runs, but only one person gets the prize? So, run to win! – 1 Corinthians 9:24 (NLT)

Of all the stories about the impact, Jim had, perhaps none better illustrates the power of positive and paying it forward than the one about Mike Bain.

He thought he wanted to be a football player for the Lebanon Warriors. At least that's what drove him to begin the ritual of the brutal two-a-day preseason practices in the blast furnace that is August in Ohio.

Football in that era was a test of manhood as much anything, and the twice-daily summer drills was a winnowing stick to measure those who didn't have what it took to be Warriors. Players immersed in football – practice in the morning, lunch, practice in the afternoon, always in full pads, lots of contact and screaming coaches whose volume knob didn't have a "mute" button. Sweat and blood were mixed with exhaustion as players pushed through high-stress drills in a setting designed to break them down, so they could be rebuilt into a team.

It only took a few practices before Bain realized he didn't measure up. As he put it, "There was everybody else on the team, and there was me."

He was a brainy kid about to enter his junior year. He stood about 6-feet tall and was a little pudgy, with essentially no athletic skill. Keeping up with the other eager varsity football players was a hopeless challenge. And he knew it.

After his mother drove him to practice one morning, he told his mother not to leave because he would be right back. There was one more ritual he had to complete, and it wouldn't take long. The coaches gathered in an office at one end of the humid, cramped locker room where players put on pads and other gear to prepare for more torture.

Bain stood in that office doorway, helmet in hand, and stared wordlessly at them. After a moment, the head coach said, "You're going to quit, aren't you?"

Bain nodded and mumbled, quietly put his helmet on the table, and started to walk away and put all this football madness behind him. As he did, he heard the sharp crack of the head coach's voice.

"Wait!"

Bain froze and turned.

"Would you want to help the team in another way?"

Bain would later say, "That was the first of several turning points where he intersected in my life."

A lot of coaches would have been glad to let someone like Bain walk out the door. Players like him only get in for a play or two in the final seconds of a 40-point rout. They can't even help that much at practice since they lack the skill to push more-talented players to get better.

So he quits. So what?

Many coaches would consider that a gift -- one less non-contributor. But Bain had a value that many others never bothered to see. A team isn't made up strictly by those who put on a uniform and perform on the field, and Vandy had an idea that would keep a young man involved.

After Bain heard the coach out, he went to the parking lot and told his mother he'd be staying at practice after all. He could help as a student manager to start. But there were even bigger plans.

Not long after, Coach VanDeGrift signed him up for a week-long course for athletic trainers at nearby Miami University. For the next two seasons, the guy who was going to quit the team instead became known as "Bainer The Trainer." His job was to help keep varsity Warriors fit and healthy enough to play, and he excelled.

They came to him with their sprained ankles, sore shoulders, knees, and backs. The more Mike Bain learned about how that process worked, the more fascinated he became with the science.

Something else was happening too. The unlikely relationship between a driven coach and the boy who became the team's student trainer thrived on trust and mutual respect. Bain was overflowing with ideas to help the Warriors when he came back from Miami. He brought his dad to the locker room to help measure for cabinets to attach to the cement walls so they could be stocked with supplies.

But he wasn't through.

The training room needed new equipment, especially an ice machine.

A football team travels on ice. Trainers use to reduce swelling on damaged joints and having an ice machine in the locker room was huge in those days. Thanks to Bain's persistence, the Warriors got one.

They also got a hydrocollator, a device to heat cloth pads. Bain convinced the coach how that machine could help him take better care of the players. Ask any aching player about the power of moist heat on sore muscles.

When an assistant coach started giving Bain a hard time about the way the training room was set up and how he was doing his job, Vandy sided with the student.

But the biggest show of faith came when Bain asked for a key so he could get into the locker room early on game days, before school started, to get things set up. Students weren't allowed to have keys to the school, for obvious reasons.

Vandy bent the rule on one condition – no one could know he had the key. It would be their secret.

"That was," Bain says now, "very significant to me."

Sure, this was about football at first. It became about much more.

The young student came to understand the coach was concerned about the kind of person he would become. Bain was always around the locker room long after the players had gone home. Coaches keep late hours too. Sometimes, Vandy and "Bainer The Trainer" were the only two left in the building.

On those occasions, this wasn't the usual student/teacher relationship. These were two human beings, talking about real issues of depth.

They would talk about school.

They would talk about his plans.

They would talk about faith.

Bain began to see the coach as someone who lived his faith authentically. He was impressed by the depth of Vandy's faith. He saw a man who about more than just reciting Bible verses and telling others how to live. Vandy had the advantage of perspective, knowing that the future would arrive for the young people around him sooner than they could imagine. He wanted them prepared.

Football was something he did with passion and dedication, but it isn't who he was. Football was a platform to affect young people in positive ways. It didn't always sound positive, though.

Mistakes in practice or a game didn't go uncorrected, and Vandy could reduce a player to jelly. The guilty player might be subjected to a tongue-lashing in front of the team at halftime during a game. It could be embarrassing and humbling.

Sometimes, after the team headed back onto the field for the second half, Vandy would ask Bain, "Do you think I was too hard on him?"

High school is a stunningly brief time, four years that flash by like orange lightning in the heat of a summer sky, but it carries implications that last a lifetime. It did so here, too. The pudgy kid who became a fixture in the LHS locker room of high-achieving athletes moved on two years later, valedictorian of his class, headed to Xavier University in Cincinnati to study chemistry.

Med school followed.

That didn't leave a lot of free time to head back to his old high school on Friday nights during football season, and Vandy had stopped coaching by then anyway. Bain's life was taken over by the need to finish residency requirements, and that's what he was doing years later at the Bethesda Hospital on the edge of the Lebanon city limits.

An old friend walked in.

It was Coach VanDeGrift.

Bain had been so wrapped up in work and studies; he hadn't heard about the fire. The deep scars on Vandy's face and hands immediately told Bain what long odds he had beaten. But there were complications. Those wounds came with a diabolical itch, which Jim scratched so hard that some of the skin grafts doctors put in place after the accident were starting to split.

The treatments doctors offered weren't helping a bit. He had worn his fingernails to the nub from scratching. His arms were raw and bleeding through his shirt, but he couldn't quit scratching.

He would scratch so hard at night, Rosie would have to sleep in another room.

Nothing helped.

There was another problem.

Vandy was days away from leaving on a long-planned trip to Europe with Rosie and several friends. The itching would ruin everything. He couldn't sleep, he couldn't sit still, and he couldn't get any relief. Taking a long plane ride under those conditions was out of the question. He was nearly ready to cancel the trip.

Could anything be done to help?

"Bainer The Trainer" invented a solution on the spot. He mixed three ingredients to make a salve. It wasn't protocol for burn victims, and a lot of doctors would have dismissed it as hopeless hogwash. But he gave it to the coach who trusted him all those years ago.

"It will either work, or your skin will fall off," Bain told the coach.

Within a couple of days, the itching stopped. The impromptu cocktail had worked.

That wasn't the only time Bain came to the rescue to someone in need.

Remember the famous Lebanon resident who lived on that 300-acre farm just outside of town and, oh yeah, also walked on the moon?

Neil Armstrong pulled off his ring finger at the knuckle one afternoon in a farming accident. He picked it up and pushed it against the nub of his finger. He was about 70 yards from his house, and he was going into shock.

He called a local dentist who was a friend because he didn't know who else to contact for help. The dentist quickly called for someone a little qualified in these situations to head over to Neil's place quickly.

It was Mike Bain. His quick action helped save the finger.

Today, the kid who was about to walk out the door and leave Jim behind forever became an executive with a large hospital company in Cincinnati. He supervises more than 50 emergency care professionals.

Single words come to Bain's mind when he thinks today of the man who changed the course of his life.

Integrity.

Compassion.

Faith.

Love.

And he thinks about what might have been if Vandy hadn't been interested enough that morning to tell him to stop before he walked out the door. Bain is a smart man with a lot of gifts, and he likely would have been a success in whatever he did.

It just might not have been medicine.

But two lives crossed at an intersection to the future that morning when the coach spoke up and stopped a young man from walking away.

Nothing has been the same.

It raises the question of what would have happened if a football coach had let Mike Bain put his helmet on the table and ride away in his mother's car. Would he be a doctor today?

The answer came without hesitation.

"I would not be, no."

CHAPTER 18: FRIENDS AND FAMILY

Do everything without complaining and arguing. – Philippians 2:14 (NLT)

Jim may have done much of his life's work out of the public eye, but the people of Lebanon also know him as a great football coach. He built the Warriors into one of the power programs of southwest Ohio while he was there. He had one losing season at Lebanon during the 15 years he was in charge.

Predictably, he made sure everyone involved with the program – players, coaches, and the wives – were part of the family.

Coaching meant daily practices during the season and endless film study of your team and the upcoming opponent. There were Sunday night meetings in the basement at Vandy's house that would run several hours. There was another long coach's meeting on Monday night. They would go until 9 p.m. or so, again on Tuesdays.

Roll the film or the tape, back and forth. Check every player. Check every block, tackle, run, or pass. Every Warrior got a grade for every down. The staff analyzed each opponent for strengths and weaknesses.

"Vandy's motto was never to leave a stone unturned," assistant coach Lee Day said.

Someone figured out that the average Lebanon football coach earned about 50 cents an hour. The other things they earned were priceless.

During the meetings, Rosie would prepare edibles like home-made Mississippi mud pie. They called it "victory treats" if they won. But if not, it was simply delicious. Dana and Jami would take the food downstairs to the guys, along with a pitcher of iced tea or lemonade. And Friday night after the game belonged to the coaches and their wives.

Everyone would meet for food, chat, and socializing. As a family, they would watch the TV for scores of the other games. Home game, road game, win or lose – it didn't matter. It brought the staff and families together as one, and all these years later they still talk about those Friday night gatherings.

The stories abound.

And Tom Hoverman likes to talk about the time when, as defensive coordinator, he took a big gamble at a critical moment of a game against their arch-rival from Franklin High School, located just miles away.

It used to be a tradition for Lebanon students to hold a huge bonfire known as the "burning of Franklin" in the middle of the week when those two football teams were about to collide.

Hoverman had joined the staff after graduating from Miami University in Oxford, Ohio. He had long hair and was wearing cut-off jeans and sandals when he met the head coach for the first time. Vandy, the man with the buzzcut hairstyle and no-nonsense demeanor, looked him up and down and went, "Oh, my goodness."

The two had forged a great relationship, though. Tom earned his stripes by preparation and attention to detail. With Lebanon clinging to a narrow lead late in the game, Franklin had the ball near midfield. For a defensive coordinator, the standard call in that situation is to protect the lead by protecting against a big play by the opponent that could cost his team the game.

Instead, Tom gambled with one of the gutsiest calls of his career to that point. He called for a goal-line defense on a critical play that left the secondary vulnerable to a long pass.

They could have lost.

That would have been bad.

Vandy saw what was happening and screamed at his coordinator on the sidelines, "What are you doing!"

Tom yelled back in the heat of the moment, "I know what they're going to do."

All that film study had convinced him Franklin was going to play it safe and run the ball. He loaded up the defense to stop that play.

Vandy gave him a look that said, "You better be right."

He was.

The defense worked. The Warriors stopped the play and won the game, which made for lively chatter afterward.

"Those days were so much fun," Kristie Hoverman said. "We were family. Tom saw the other coaches more than us, but I loved football season and those special people."

A party for the coaches and supporters and a chance to unwind seems like a small thing. That wasn't the only way to keep the family feeling going.

Rosie and Jim would stage a mini Olympics for the coaches and wives before the school year started. They set up a course with all kinds of events for the couples, followed, of course, by a buffet complete with Rosie's homegrown food.

It was one way to keep football in perspective with life.

There was another way, too.

It was accepted practice at that time to hold twice-daily practices in full pads, one in the morning, and one in the afternoon, with lots of contact, in the blast furnace of August heat. It was a winnowing stick for coaches to learn who had the goods and who didn't, but it also would wear players to the bone. On one broiling afternoon, there had been an unusual amount of complaining, and that was something Vandy wouldn't allow. So, after the morning practice, he ordered his players to load on to buses. They took a side trip to a nearby home for mentally disabled children.

The football players came face to face with kids less fortunate than them. They saw how those kids lived. And they stopped complaining about the heat and screaming coaches.

The lesson was clear: You're just playing a game, but for these kids, this is a reality.

CHAPTER 19: A SPECIAL SEASON

***The horse is prepared for the day
of battle, but the victory belongs
to the Lord. – Proverbs 21:31 (NLT)***

You can't talk about Lebanon football in the VanDeGrift era without the 1980 season. That's the year the Warriors were 12-0 and headed to the Ohio Class II state championship game.

The town was awash in excitement. It seemed like every storefront in town had a "Go Warriors" sign on display, painted in maroon and white of course. People were making their plans to travel to Columbus, the state capital, against Youngstown Cardinal Mooney, a Catholic high school and a traditional powerhouse. The matchup was straight from the movies: a public school from a small town against the private school juggernaut from a larger city.

But even as the townspeople celebrated and dreamed of a victorious finish to a dream season, Jim – ever the realist - knew what was going to happen. He had known since he put on the first roll of Cardinal Mooney film.

That team outweighed the Warriors by at least 20 pounds or more per man. It was faster. Stronger. Mooney had seven players who would sign Division I-A college scholarships and some went on to professional careers. Several underclassmen eventually would play college ball too.

On top of that, some of Lebanon's key players were injured and limping for the game. Running back Eddie Fugett, so key to the offense, was struggling. Linebacker Jim Stone was hurt. Tight end Tom Shoop was hurt. Ty, the quarterback, and kicker had an aching back. Kelly Addison had a knee injury. Scott Brown was struggling.

Yeah, it was going to be a challenge, even if the Warriors were completely healthy. Everyone knew that.

After watching just a few minutes of the film in the basement at his home, though, the head coach had a firm grasp on what his team was about to face. It was simple. Rosie wouldn't have to prepare victory treats after this one. They had no shot.

No amount of coaching, pleading, driving, or pushing could change that. Mooney wasn't just better; it was a lot better.

It's over, Vandy said to no one in particular. It was a lonely feeling. He turned off the projector and went to bed.

It was 1:30 a.m.

Until that moment of realization, the season had been the stuff about which small town players, coaches, and fans dream. It had been from the start. There had been a noticeable difference as the football team the head coach and his staff assembled began preparations for that season. Ohio had expanded the playoffs for the first time, creating more classes of schools to allow smaller programs like Lebanon to have a chance to compete on a statewide level.

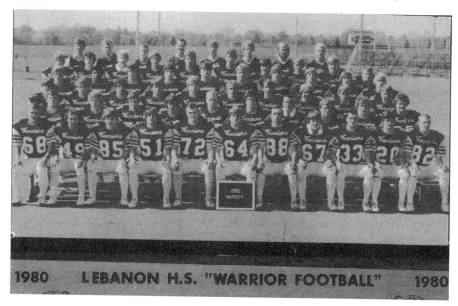

1980   LEBANON H.S. "WARRIOR FOOTBALL"   1980

The Warriors expected to be good; by then, they always expected to be good. Two years before, they had finished 10-0 and surrendered only two touchdowns all season. Even that wasn't good enough to qualify for the playoffs under the old formula.

The 1980 season was going to be different.

It wasn't going to be easy, though. Senior offensive guard Tim Bashford noticed before the season even began that, at 180 pounds, he was 10 or 20 pounds lighter, at least, than most offensive linemen of his day – but he also was the Warriors' third-biggest player. Collectively, the Warriors averaged 173 pounds per man.

No excuses, though. That's not the VanDeGrift way. He pounded a mantra from the First Book of Things Football Coaches Say into the team – "Luck is When Preparation Meets Opportunity."

Through preparation, there would be the opportunity to overcome whatever deficiencies that might have seemed apparent on the first glance.

What they couldn't do through talent or preparation, they

made up for by knocking the ever-lovin' tar out of opponents. They were the hardest-hitting team to ever suit up for Lebanon at that point.

Their names were almost interchangeable: Stone, Lester, Gilbert, Branan, Tolliver, Norris, Collins, Addison, Groh, Roarke, Brown, Shoop – neighborhood kids who grew up on Warrior football and could sing the words to Onward Lebanon from the bottom of their souls.

They were almost always in the right position, especially in Tom Hoverman's defense – that renowned attention to detail the head coach instilled in his staff – and when they made contact, they made sure the opposing player felt it.

That attitude had been drilled into the players since they first suited up in the fourth grade in Lebanon's pee-wee feeder system. They ran many of the same drills there they would run as Warriors. They ran the same plays.

When they reached the varsity, position coaches Hoverman, Rich Pare, Lee Day and Jim Norris reinforced the basics.

It takes more than fundamentals, hard hits, and clever plays to make a championship team, though. It takes a special inner something, a sense that the team is bigger than the sum of its collective parts.

It hard to describe and can't be manufactured, only felt. Teams know when it's there, and when it isn't.

For this team, it was there. Everyone had a part.

There were deep friendship and a sense of purpose by everyone in maroon and white. There was accountability. And while the roster may not have overflowed with players that made the eyes of college scouts light up, they had some football players.

Fugett piled up yardage. Ty ran the offensive efficiently. Players like Bashford, Jeff Collins, and Scott Dye didn't mind getting their noses bloodied if it meant the difference between winning and losing.

And it all came together.

They swept through the first nine games of the regular season without a loss. Most of the games weren't close. They didn't talk about playoffs much, but the Warriors were in the picture.

Teams qualified for the playoffs by a complicated computer formula, and most didn't try to figure it out. But Ty did. After games, he would go through the scores around the state and compute Lebanon's chances of making the field.

If the Warriors kept winning, the numbers were in their favor. But there was one huge obstacle remaining – unbeaten rival Edgewood High, about 20 miles away in Trenton, Ohio, in week 10. It was for the league championship. It was for a playoff berth.

You never know who will step up in a big game, but it's safe to say people would never have believed Andy Russell would be that guy. He was a senior, 125 pounds at most.

That's ten more pounds than he weighed as a sophomore, though.

"When coach asked how much I weighed, and I told him 115 pounds, I saw the look on his face," Russell said. "I told him I didn't care if I was 100 pounds. I wasn't backing down."

He was a cornerback and safety on defense, and on a good night, he might get into the game for a couple of plays.

He had stuck it out for three years, though, and no one got cut from the team if they showed up, did the work, and followed the rules. Russell's main contribution was on the scout team; that's made up of backup players who simulate the opponents' offense and defense. Twice, he had been named Scout Player of the Week.

He was the essence of the kind of program the head coach had sought to build – tough, competitive, but inclusive. Everyone in the room was a Warrior.

Since Edgewood was the final regular-season game of their careers, seniors got a chance to address the team. From here on out, it was sudden death for the Warriors; one loss and it was over.

Even though he knew he wouldn't play a minute, Andy Russell was not going to let his team lose.

He was the last of the seniors to speak.

"I guess that's fitting since I'm the least of those in here," Russell told the assembled players as they listened quietly. "I don't know what I'm doing here. I'm not big enough. I'm not strong enough. I'm not fast enough. Coach VanDeGrift let me be on this team.

"I've only gotten into a couple of games, but I wouldn't trade this for the world. It makes me somebody to walk the hallways at school on game days wearing that jersey and to be on the sidelines with my brothers. I'm not ready for this to be over, guys. We have to win!"

Tears began to fill the eyes of many in that room.

From that moment on, Edgewood had no chance.

The Warriors were Mid-Miami League champions.

A week later, they beat Roth High School in Dayton 17-0 in Lebanon's first playoff game ever.

A lot of people didn't believe that was supposed to happen.

Roth had a running back named Keith Byars, who would become an All-American at Ohio State. He finished second in Heisman Trophy balloting. He became a celebrated player for Philadelphia and Miami in the National Football League. The Warriors shut him down.

Shut him down?

It was a rout. It was that way on both sides of the ball.

When Ty ran for two touchdowns, he was escorted into the end zone by his offensive line.

The Warriors throttled Columbus Watterson 29-7 to win a berth in the state championship game. The score didn't reflect the beating they took, though. Ty remembers thinking Watterson had been the most physical team he had ever faced.

And now, here they were.

Little ol' Leb-nun was in the state championship game.

The coach might have a strong idea of what was about to happen to his team in the title game, but he didn't let it show to the players or staff. Preparation was normal. Sure, Mooney was good, but the Warriors expected to play well because their coach told them he expected them to. They expected to win.

Oh, it was an awful night.

They had scrape four inches of snow and ice off the field before kickoff. The temperature hovered around 20 degrees, made worse by a swirling 14-mile-per-hour wind that sliced through clothing layers like the business end of an icepick.

In the stands that night, Fred Boulton - Vandy's defensive coordinator for seven seasons and one of his closest friends thought, "How can you play football in this weather?"

You can if the game is for the state championship.

As Ty settled under center at quarterback to take the team's first offensive snap, he yelled in the direction of the Mooney defenders, "Lebanon Warriors are Number One!"

And from the other side of the field came a smirking and profane response that, loosely translated, said, "No, you're not."

Jeff Norris, who was playing receiver that night for the Warriors, remembered thinking, "I'm looking up and down the line, and they're bigger than us at every position, and they looked pretty mean, and I'm like, "Ty, shut up! Don't make 'em mad!"

Alas, the things Jim saw on film came to life on that frozen field.

The dream was over.

Shortly after the game began, Tim Bashford was knocked silly by a hard hit from a Mooney player. He had played organized football since the fourth grade and was never hit that hard.

It was foreshadowing.

Boulton, who had moved into administration at LHS, had watched some film on Mooney during that week with Vandy and drew the same conclusion.

"The talent they had was so evenly distributed across the whole team," he said. "Mooney had good athletes at every position. We were physically overmatched. They were so big and strong."

Near the end of the first half, the Warriors trailed 13-0 but had the ball at Mooney's 3-yard line. A touchdown would cut the lead in half, maybe supply some needed momentum for the final two quarters.

A penalty knocked Lebanon back 5 yards, though, leaving Ty to attempt a short field goal. He was a reliable kicker, but he was still dealing with the remnants of the pounding the Warriors had taken the week before against Watterson. Ty had taken blows to his back in that game, and it left him unable to extend his leg to kick fully.

His field goal attempt was blocked.

It came apart in the final two quarters. A couple of passes were picked off and returned for touchdowns. The task of trying to contain the larger, faster opponent finally wore the Warriors down. Some of them wobbled to the sidelines, unable to continue.

They trudged back to the locker room with a 50-0 defeat that made a frigid night seem arctic.

Through it all, Bashford remembered the tone set by his head coach and how it filtered through the staff. There was only encouragement to keep playing hard. Never give up. Even when it became obvious that they were not going to win, keep playing.

"We stuck it out to the bitter end," Bashford said. "And I never saw the coaches show any other emotion than for us to keep at it."

In the locker room afterward, there were tears and hugs. They knew they were saying goodbye to a special chapter in their lives. There were words of thanks. It was quiet. Disappointment shrouded the room--for the team, for the town. But sometimes, coaches do their best jobs in situations like that, and their leader had a message to share: There is no disgrace in losing to a better team if you didn't quit.

The Warriors could walk out that night with their heads high. They hadn't quit. That was all their coach had asked. The togetherness they had was memorialized 25 years later when the team went into the Lebanon High Hall of Fame as a group.

Some of them hadn't been back to town since the fire that nearly killed their coach. Some of those still in town, like Andy Russell, hadn't had a chance to talk with him. Those boys were men now, with responsibilities and families.

How would Vandy look? What had the fire taken from him?

They soon found out.

"The minute Coach opened his mouth; it was still him," Bashford said.

The humbleness. The gratitude. Appreciation. It was all right there in Vandy's voice.

High school football isn't just about plays, practice, and victory parties. It's about lessons that carry boys into adulthood. Their coach would tell them, "If you're not all over the details, you'll never make it."

He preached follow-up.

Follow-through.

Proper execution.

Everyone was part of the family, but that came with responsibilities. It's like Vandy's dad told him all those years ago, put that shovel in your hand.

Vandy today smiles at the memory of how his team of over-achievers collectively rose above themselves.

The group had a rare togetherness -- players, coaches, parents, cheerleaders, even townspeople. Everyone seemed to under-stand something special was about to happen, and everyone had a responsibility to make sure it did.

That spirit of togetherness was what Vandy had set out to build in his football program.

But there is one other thought about that season, one not dulled by time or distance.

The final game.

50-0.

It was a long time ago. Jim knew Lebanon couldn't win because his team was out-matched. The Warriors could have played a perfect game and likely would still have lost. Maybe it would have, could have, and all things equal, should have been closer, but the scoreboard remains the same. The competitor will never forget.

Surprise you?

It shouldn't.

CHAPTER 20: THE SKY WEPT

Love each other with genuine affection and take delight in honoring each other. – Romans 12:10 (NLT)

The sky was weeping on that bone-chilling October night in 1997, barely four months after Jim wasn't supposed to live through the night when the townspeople of Lebanon gathered to honor the man they loved and almost lost.

Do you say the sky can't take on human characteristics and express emotion? Scientists can argue that point, but science also had determined Jim would be dead before the sun rose on the morning after the accident. And if technically that was icy rain falling from the sky on a night that was the harbinger of the approaching winter, well, there were plenty of real tears from everyone there to witness the dedication of James VanDeGrift Stadium, home of the Lebanon Warriors.

Naming the field for the coach who put Lebanon football on the map should have been a formality, and many knew they would get around to it one day, once they were able to settle on the right way to honor their coach. A new high school, presumably with a new stadium, was in the works and a lot of people supported the idea of waiting until it was ready to formalize what everyone felt and knew about Vandy.

The problem is that new school was still on the drawing board. It didn't open for another seven years. They never did build another football stadium, either, for what that's worth.

Whatever the obstacles, they melted away in the aftermath of the accident. The dedication would be on Oct. 24, 1997 -- 16 years after he had stepped away from the sideline. It's easy to say the fire forced Lebanon's hand, but some people say that's not so.

"His injury shouldn't have anything to do with it because it's what he did while coach of the Warriors that earned this honor," David Brausch, who was Lebanon's coach in 1997, told the Western Star.

"But I'm human enough to know that there are people out there who will think (that's why) we're doing this. I know Vandy well enough to know that he wouldn't want this because of that. This is something he earned during his 15-year stint as head coach of the Warriors."

Fans filled the stands on that late October night and pressed against a chain-link fence ringing the field. There weren't just football fans either. Nurses and therapists who helped in Vandy's recovery were in the crowd, and on any other night, many fans would have stayed home warm and dry.

Jim took a risk by coming and on a night like this because he would feel the weather's effects more than anyone else. He was still in recovery from his wounds, and he had lost multiple layers of skin in the fire. Even with the grafts, covered by multiple layers of clothing and a compression suit to keep him warm, the night was frighteningly cold to him.

He was shaking and shivering as the persistent rain reflected in the stadium lights while he waited in a wheelchair under an umbrella for the ceremony to begin.

A small plaque attached to a post at the front gate was the only visible sign of the name change. It had been a rush job, and close friends of Vandy, including Don Colston and Ron Holtrey, argued someone of Vandy's stature deserved better. Colston later led a

Joe Henderson

fund-raising drive to replace the post with a large granite monument that reminds every fan entering the stadium why Jim Van-DeGrift matters.

It reads:

"Jim VanDeGrift molded a generation of young men. Through his dedication to his coaching, education, God, his family, Lebanon High School, and the community, he influenced many lives. He is an example and an inspiration to youth unparalleled in the history of Lebanon Athletics."

Everyone that night understood why they were there, whether they were from Lebanon or for the other team. After everything they had been through together, the saga needed an emphatic statement, and this was it. It was one more chance for Lebanon to wrap its arms around this good man, its best friend, and say, emphatically, we love you.

The ceremony was supposed to be brief, and Vandy was supposed to stay in the chair, say a few words of appreciation, and head someplace warm. People weren't prepared for what happened next, though.

He rose from the chair.

Say again -- he got out of the chair.

That should have been miracle enough for one night. Nothing, not even something like he had been through, was going to keep him down. But he wasn't standing still; he had a purpose in mind. He took off across the wet, muddy field. Some say he was running, and others say it was more of a shuffle.

Whatever it was, glory be! By that time, the sky wasn't the only thing crying.

Players and coaches from both teams stood locked on the sidelines. To Vandy, they were what people came to see.

He spoke to the Warriors. Then the man who at first wasn't supposed to be alive, and then wasn't supposed to be walking, made

141

the trip across the field and apologized to the players from Goshen High School for making them wait through something like this.

Of course, he would do that. He wasn't kidding, either. He would never want to interfere with a football game, especially if that interference was because people were making a fuss about him. But this was a fuss?

Be serious.

There were tears -- God would have to count them all for us to know how many fell that night, seeking cover in the autumn rain. But what were those tears saying?

Many things.

They were expressions of love.

Awe.

Praise.

As Pastor Bill Cain would later say, "I have read of miracles in the Bible, and there were very few of them. I would classify what happened with him as a miracle."

And Jeff Norris, the player, said plainly, "Would I call it a miracle? I would."

Through her free-flowing tears that night, daughter Dana learned something that will stick with her forever.

"It completely opened my eyes to the beauty of a community like ours," she said.

What happened in those four months was much more than former football players supporting an old coach. There was a lot of that, to be sure, but many of those constant prayers and bended knees came from students, friends, acquaintances, rivals, or just people who had this man enter their lives on a mission of goodness.

There was the steady parade of visitors to the hospital, many of whom never actually got to see him but came anyway, to be near him. There were the angels who made meals appear for the family, or took turns holding their hands, or got them out of the hospital for a few hours of normal. Vicky Barnthouse, an administrator, and nurse who helped care for Vandy, said she had never before seen so many cards on the hospital windows and walls as there were for him.

Naming the stadium in Jim's honor was just the next phase of the love fest.

The Warriors won that game 49-8 to complete an undefeated regular season. A year later, the Warriors won Ohio's Class II state championship.

The timing seemed appropriate.

It was the first full season played in James VanDeGrift Stadium, and 18 years after Cardinal Mooney.

A generation had passed since he stood on Lebanon's sideline, time enough for those who knew him best to age, or move away, or to put the lessons he taught them on the football field into real-life practice.

But that monument remains at the front gate with his name, reminding everyone who enters in about the man who started it all. It will stay there for as long as the Warriors do.

Yes, the sky was crying on that October night. Don't bother trying to tell anyone who was there that it wasn't, because they know better.

Tears of joy? It seems likely.

CHAPTER 21: THE RIPPLES OF A MIRACLE

And we know that God causes everything to work together] for the good of those who love God and are called according to his purpose for them. --- Romans 8:28 (NLT)

Time is a great agent of change. It can erode old habits and reshape long-held attitudes. Big things become little things. Things that once seemed important give way to new realizations and priorities. For most people, such things happen gradually over a lifetime.

It's fair to say Vandy was on his way to such changes long before the accident. As a young football coach, for instance, he was driven to the point of obsession. Practices were long, and breaks were few. It was the standard of the day in the sport.

He could be more than a bit obsessive, too.

During lunch periods, for instance, players were given the option of having fruit – apples, oranges, or bananas. Banana peels went into the trash, but the coach had better not find a discarded apple core or orange peel. That was a sign of waste.

He would check, too.

One of his players remembered how one day after practice coach had a grasshopper in his hand. Grinning, he looked at some of the guys and said, "Let me show you what to do this with."

He bit off the grasshopper's head.

He did that a lot. It was one of those things football people did. Don't ask why. He said he once bit off a mouse head, too, "But I spit it out."

Players expected their mistakes to be corrected, um, enthusiastically. Often that involved a hard slap to the shoulder pads or upside the helmet, or he would grab the player's facemask to get their attention.

His longtime friend and former assistant, Fred Boulton, recalled, "When he stared holes through you with those big blue eyes of his, you felt 2-feet tall."

Even though there is no hint that his motivational techniques ever crossed the line, things have changed. The game has changed. There's a good chance today stuff like that would wind up in headlines. The players of Vandy's era just accepted it as part of the package with football.

He looks back on that person now with a mix of disbelief and amazement. He certainly would change a lot of his tactics. He would tell the young Vandy to relax more, to take it easy.

A little bit anyway.

But the slowly evolving changes in outlook and priorities hit the jet stream after the fire.

"You could see him emerge from this a different man," Bill Cain said. "His soul was changed. There was a renewed sense of intentionality that focused on Christ and what had been done for him. He had been given the gift of life, and he knew he had to use it for others.

"He was a man of God before all that, but I had never seen the depth in him before that I saw after the fire."

Tom Russell, his former player and assistant coach, noticed the biggest change in the weeks and months following the fire after the immediate danger had passed.

There was softening of the rough edges, maybe because the accident forced him to let others take control. As a head coach, he had always been in charge. He was comfortable with giving gruff commands and telling tired and bleeding players that they had to try harder.

Now, he needed the help of doctors, his wife, family, friends, and those he didn't know even cared about him.

Russell heard it in Vandy's voice.

"He never understood how many people cared about him and his family," he said. "The community told him, 'We're not going to let you go.' Once he understood that, things changed."

His wife, Rosie, noticed it too.

She had lived for decades with a tough, demanding man who wanted things done a specific way.

Now?

"He doesn't fuss as much about things like that," Rosie said. "He was always such a tough guy and pretty rigid. Now he sees the value of life a little more clearly."

Kristie Hoverman saw it. She has a long-term perspective. She was junior at LHS and a varsity cheerleader when Vandy took over as head coach. As a coach's wife, she understood the highs and lows of the game. There were good times after wins, and maybe some recovery time after losses.

She saw the driven coach.

And she saw the changes.

"Jim always tried to be in control of everything he possibly could be, so his high expectations could achieve all that was possible in every area of his life. All of a sudden this strong and proud man had no control, and lay in pain, not knowing if he would live," she said.

"I remember that one of his first questions after the accident was 'Am I going to die?' I listened to him talk about that time, and he had no fear of dying and knew where he would be going. Even though the family wanted him to remain here with them, the trust they displayed was such a witness.

"I've heard him talk about his dependence on the strength he received every minute and hour. God couldn't change his circumstance, but He gave him the courage, strength, power to persevere through those agonizing days. And it was evident God supplied the same for Rosie."

As close as Mark Armstrong was with Ty and the VanDeGrift family, he never played football – golf was his best sport.

He regrets the missed opportunity to this day, but the lessons he learned from the coach he never played for still resonate.

"Coach had an uncanny ability to see potential in people, and not just on the football field," Armstrong said. "But he did more than just see it; he helped a lot of them find that potential inside them.

"I know many of them that he touched, inspired, and helped them find a path."

By his admission, Vandy was an irregular visitor to friends or acquaintances who were in the hospital before the accident. No longer. That's especially true when a burn victim could use a visit.

His survival didn't guarantee personal comfort, though. He doesn't talk about this much, if at all, but years later he remains trapped in a body that still rebels against the effects of the accident.

His morning ritual for the rest of his life will include exercises to stretch the skin around his neck, arms, and other parts of his body. He continues to have regular surgeries to battle the long-term effects. He doesn't talk about that much to anyone.

But he has done more than survive a catastrophe. He found renewed purpose in the life he kept.

Maybe that's part of the mission God gave him on June 5, 1997.

Who better to give comfort and hope than someone who has gone through the flames and understands what's at stake?

CHAPTER 22: YOU NEVER REALLY LEAVE

No, despite all these things, overwhelming victory is ours through Christ, who loved us.
– Romans 8:37 (NLT)

There was a surprise party on the night of June 5, 2017. It was the 20th anniversary of the day a blown gasoline cap sent Jim's life, and that of his family and friends in a direction none could have imagined.

He knew that day was the anniversary, as he does every June 6.

"I'll always have a recollection on that day, but I usually push it aside," he said. "They aren't real fond memories."

This June 5 was different, though. He didn't know that his family had gathered along with first responders, therapists, nurses, doctors, and others who played a role in his recovery. He and Ty had slipped out that afternoon to visit a friend, but it was part of the subterfuge.

On the way home, Ty said they needed to stop by his sister Jami's house. There were some extra cars, but Jim paid them no heed until he walked in the door and was caught flat-footed by the greeting he received.

They shared stories of his recovery, and those dark days after the accident. But they also laughed, maybe cried a little bit, but mostly they just enjoyed the fellowship that comes with living.

His body still bears the scars and other reminders of what happened. There are also some side effects beyond the obvious. Skin grafts covered much of his body, but the new skin doesn't give the same sensation or feel that normal skin does. It has no sweat glands. He gets cold even in the summer and sleeps with extra blankets. He can't feel rain pelt off his arms, and he'll never be able to fully straighten his left arm – a problem, given that he is left-handed.

Vandy is as alive and vibrant as ever, though.

You can call it a miracle of medicine, a miracle of the Divine, or maybe a merger of the two. He had great medical care throughout his recovery but ask anyone, and they'll tell you about a town that stayed on its knees for weeks and begged God to let him stay.

His survival is only part of this story. It was not merely a happy ending. In many ways, it was a happy beginning that made a man, his family, and a small Ohio town understand the value of community better than they ever had.

This is not a nomination for sainthood. Everybody has critics, and there was a time when he was an acquired taste. His direct, demanding, never-yielding, seeming all-out devotion to winning at everything didn't always go over well. He could be intimidating, at least until people figured out that he always put a premium on helping others realize what they were capable of doing.

The fire helped many of those understand the adage of paying it forward as the only way to properly thank Jim for what he had done for them. His example became the blueprint repay that debt by helping others.

The fire also put him on a platform he had previously resisted as he came to realize he had a story to tell about faith and endurance and he began to share that in churches, clubs, and any meeting or place where people asked him to speak.

Before the fire, he was an infrequent visitor to people in the hospital. Afterward, he looked for chances to make those visits and share a word of encouragement about life and faith. There is no way to calculate the ripples that went forth from the sharing.

Maybe that's the point.

Life isn't football.

It doesn't come with a scoreboard to total the wins and losses. Sharing and caring is about community, not personal glory. Vandy became even more obedient about heeding the call to service on a deeper level. The effect of those visits, well, who can say for sure. That's between those people and God.

The point is being willing to try.

People must have noticed.

He only told a few people – family, mostly - when he learned he was to be inducted into the Ohio High School Football Hall of Fame. Few people in Lebanon and even fewer around the state knew of the honor he was about to receive. It's his way. He doesn't go looking for parades. By the way, that's one of seven Halls of which is a member, including for basketball officiating. Word got around about the football honor, and because of who he is many of his coaching peers from all over traveled to the ceremony to show support.

The recovery was long and painful in ways that can be gruesome. Burn victims are especially vulnerable to infection, and Vandy fought his share of those.

He is still here.

The aftermath of the fire helped showcase medical advances in the treatment of severe burn victims. A surgical mask produced by a team of researchers helped reduce scarring and was considered a leap forward at the time.

Why did something like this happen to such a good man?

Many people were confronting God with that question in the days and weeks after the fire. Does God cause these things? Could God have stopped it? More to the point, should God have stopped it?

That's a debate for theologians. Here is a point beyond dispute, though: God can use these events to spread a wider message.

Jim is proof.

Living proof.

It doesn't solve the mystery why some prayers are answered in situations like this while others seemingly aren't. It's a question Dana admits she has pondered often.

Without the fire, Vandy would have been just as beloved in Lebanon, maybe living out his days in quiet satisfaction but relative anonymity. His story would have spread no further than the city limits until it gradually faded from memory. Instead, he went through fire and came out on the other side. He has been where few people have.

Because of that, who can say with any certainty how far the ripples of his story have reached?

Everyone, it seems, has a memory to share about their coach and friend, and collectively they paint a total picture of the man.

Ty's friend, Troy Holtrey, remembered meeting someone outside a shoe store more than two and a half years after Troy's father died. The man asked if he was related to Ron Holtrey, and they struck up a conversation. He talked about a recent chance encounter with Jim, where the man asked him about Ron. The wound from the loss opened fresh. Jim started crying right there in public.

That's just one of an endless number of tales of Jim's humanity and kindness.

Lee Day came to Lebanon as an assistant coach, via the Ohio Northern pipeline. He didn't have a place to stay when he arrived, though, so Vandy and Rosie put him up in the basement of their home until he got settled. They did the same for a lot of people.

Jim stays involved in sports in many ways. He spent many years as a broadcaster for LHS athletic events over cable's Lebanon Channel. He hosted a weekly sports show highlighting Warrior athletics. That's how Lebanon's younger generation and new residents probably know him best today.

Even then, the renowned VanDeGrift determination showed through.

Years after the accident, he developed a staph infection from his wounds. He didn't know that at first, but he did know he wasn't feeling well.

There was a Friday night game at Beavercreek, about a 45-minute drive from Lebanon. He shouldn't have gone to cover the game, but he did anyway.

Spence Cropper remembers it was bad. After the game, Jim said he wasn't sure he could even make it down the stadium steps. In the car, he sat with his eyes closed and saying nothing. He had an open wound and a fever.

When they finally got him to accept medical help, doctors said he could have died from the infection.

Tom Russell, a former player and assistant coach for Jim, remembers the car rides to and from games after the fire. Vandy was given drugs by doctors to suppress some of the worst memories of the fire. Snippets of what happened come back slowly.

In those rides along Ohio state highways, Russell had plenty of time to talk. A lot of times it was about the events of the day – school, sports, politics, whatever.

When it gets around to the fire and his recovery, some of his memories are still vague. But one isn't.

"It always comes back to, 'I didn't know how many people cared,'" Russell said.

Vandy has a reputation with his friends of being frugal, but that doesn't stop him from reaching into his wallet and giving money to someone in need, sometimes a stranger.

He was good enough to coach football at the college level. So why didn't he? Bill Robinson, his old position coach at Ohio Northern, had the answer.

"He wasn't ready to make that commitment," he said. "He is a small-town guy. He was very happy where he was. He made a home in Lebanon, and that was good enough."

Jim knew college coaching was a business, and even good coaches are fired for things beyond their control. He didn't want that. He liked stability. He wanted to make a difference.

Society has been disappointed by the behavior of so many leaders and athletes who claim Christianity but live lives a life of convenience. Rosie and Jim are the real things. So are Ty, Jami, and Dana. They live victorious lives. Their families live victorious lives. Their friends do the same.

They are a modern-day adaptation of The Waltons, that 1970s TV series about a family with over-reaching love for each other. It shouldn't surprise anyone that they're all athletic, too – right down to the grandkids.

Ty and Mary's daughter, Grace, was a standout distance runner at the University of Florida. Their son, Trey, was a quarterback for an unbeaten Durant High team in Tampa and graduated from the U.S. Air Force Academy, like his Aunt Jami and Uncle Tom. He now is an officer and pilot and married his high school sweetheart, Jenna Weir.

Daughter Amery made her mark in tennis and volleyball and works for the football program at the University of Florida.

Jami and Tom's kids were the same. Maria went to Stanford on a track scholarship and married Ian Collins from Lebanon. Hanah played lacrosse in high school and at Lee University, where she was co-captain of the team. Roselen plays lacrosse at the Air Force Academy. The youngest, T.J., is a promising all-conference football player at Moeller High School in Cincinnati and also is a standout lacrosse player.

Don't forget Dana and Spence's three daughters. Josie played volleyball and basketball for the Warriors. Sophia was a distance runner in cross country who follows the example set by Grace. Lily is an excels in volleyball. Each girl is creative in the arts like their mom.

They are reflections of what they were taught, and by what they saw.

Earl Daniel told how Vandy would mow the grass every Saturday at the local Head Start building. Daniel's mother lived nearby at the elderly center. Vandy would always stop mowing and wave to her because he knew she would hear the mower and look at the window for him. Often he brought her fresh vegetables from their garden.

Jim has become Lebanon's encourager-in-chief – and not just for Warrior athletes. Marty Egleston, a long-time friend, told of his first encounter with the man. It was at a cross-country meet where Egleston's daughter competed for another school. She had lost the race and was extremely disappointed.

"I remember Jim going up to her and telling her, 'Don't you ever give up. You're a great runner.' This man is not like an ordinary coach. I've rarely seen a coach go up to another runner and do something like that," he said.

"But once you know him and you've shared experiences with him, the things he does will never leave you."

As many random acts of kindness as he gives, though, he never forgets when he is on the receiving end. Kristie Hoverman told of sending him a copy of the Serenity Prayer during his recovery. Now Jim carries that whenever he gives a talk.

He also serves as the truant officer for Lebanon schools, to keep kids from dropping out.

"I always said that the reason he is such a good truant officer is that he learned all their tricks when he was a student," his brother Faren said. "He could test the limit of the rules when he was in high school."

There are so many other aspects of this man and his family. For the final word, though, let's fall back on one of Vandy's favorite sayings: Walk it like you talk it.

The man talked it, walked it, and walks it still.

At 78 years old, he joined Rosie, his sister Myra Jean and brother-in-law John Paulus on an 11-day mission trip to Africa. It started with a flight to Chicago, then a 13-hour flight to Hamad International Airport in Doha, Qatar, followed by a 6-hour flight to Nairobi, and finally an 8-hour drive deep into northern Kenya on rock-hard worn seats in a rickety mini-bus.

They journeyed along some pothole-riddled dirt roads, their trip interrupted by the occasional baboon, zebra, herds of cattle, or just people who used the path as a walkway. They stayed at a primitive motel in a 10-by-12-foot room that bad to be covered by mosquito netting.

Sometimes the lights and water would work. Sometimes, they wouldn't.

The daily diet consisted of white rice, tortillas, and boiled eggs, and the days were filled with trips to remote villages or prisons to pass out supplies. Eyeglasses are prized, even used ones, and Jim had collected about 200 pair in advance of the trip. They were all gone in a couple of days.

So were the special Bibles they bought, printed in English and

Swahili. People held them like they were gold bars from Fort Knox. The travelers noticed something else, too. During the evening worship services, people who had so little materially were overflowing with inner joy in praise of the Lord.

That image stuck with Jim.

"I have this need to see things for myself," he said. "You can read about it in a book or see it on TV, but when you see something yourself, it stays with you. That's why I've always tried to visit places. I know what the Garden of Gethsemane looks like because I've been there. I know what the path Jesus walked to the cross is like because I walked it. That's what I took away with from Africa. It's one thing to hear about the people there but seeing them, and the way they live takes it to a higher level."

CHAPTER 23: A LIFE OF COMMITMENT

Is anything too hard for the Lord? – Genesis 18:14 (NLT)

Bill Cain, the minister, has a blue silk necktie with a gold manger scene, a Christmas gift from the VanDeGrifts. He wears it under his robe every year when he preaches a Christmas Eve sermon.

He shares the familiar story of the Christmas miracle of a birth in Bethlehem, of course, but he also frequently tells of another miracle he witnessed first-hand. He pulls the tie from under his robe and tells of a man, horribly burned, and not expected to live. He talks of a family's unending faith and the town that prayed alongside them.

He talks about believing the unbelievable.

"With God, nothing is impossible," he tells them. "When God makes up His mind to do something, He does it."

Cain has shared that story at services attended by more than 3,000 people and at civic club gatherings attended by only a handful. The small-town football coach who wanted nothing more than to lift others has reached untold thousands of people with a message of hope and faith in the worst of circumstances.

He tells them, and they tell others, and the telling likely helped other burn victims find hope in a time of trial.

There were many stories in the newspapers and on TV, including one about a year after the accident in the New York Times. The story told how, "He (Vandy) landed in a hospital where a group of engineers, doctors, and physical therapists was experimenting with movie-industry technology to produce a facial mask that they hoped would help him heal faster and reduce the need for surgery."

Researchers used 3-D surface scanning to get a hyper-accurate map of the face. It replaced the old technique of making a plaster mold, which was painful, claustrophobic, and not always effective.

Vandy proved to be the perfect patient, and the things researchers learned from him helped expedite treatment of thousands of burn victims, including firefighters. The American Burn Association estimates there are approximately 40,000 burn victims annually, and about 30,000 of those are serious enough to require admission to a hospital's specialized burn unit.

The ripples of the event swept up Vandy, too.

He became, in Cain's words, "more intentional" about sharing his faith.

"I saw a man who had faith in Jesus Christ before the accident," he said. "But now, there was a stand-up – let me tell you about Jesus. This is a life that has touched many other lives."

That intentionality was evident when Jim joined Rosie and walked to the front of the Presbyterian Church about six months after the fire.

It was supposed to be a brief thank-you to the members and friends who supported the family in so many ways in the weeks and months that followed the accident. It wound up being a 15-minute testimony to healing and service, spoken through choked voices and received with moistened eyes.

Everyone in the pews that morning had served in some way; with meals, blood donations, or just holding hands and praying. It's just what good people do. A lot of times, they don't grasp how important those things are, even the small things.

"What would have been like without him? That's a deep hole," Kelly Pickworth said. "You don't expect coach to die. There's not anyone I can think of that means more to Lebanon than Jim VanDeGrift. He's the old oak tree of this community."

Who knows how many lives were impacted by the ripples of his survival? When it's someone you know and care about, you don't see or hear about something like that without being changed.

Bob Peeler, the prosecutor-turned-judge who happened by the accident site on that warm June afternoon, remembers the frustration of not having a blanket in his car to help put out the flames. He now carries one in his trunk, just in case. He occasionally sees Vandy when they work out at the local YMCA and marvels how a man 16 years older than him, who has endured what Vandy did, "Is in much better shape than me."

Earl Daniel remembers staring through the 4-x-4 window in Vandy's room at ICU, knowing how serious it was, wondering how anyone could survive that, and later being awestruck that he did.

"I came to understand that God had a plan," he said.

That's as good a way as any to explain this.

If he had died that day in the fire, the only newspaper stories would have been on the obituary pages. The only gathering at the church would have been for a funeral. Perhaps the football stadium would still bear his name, but the dedication would have been somber instead of a celebration.

Cain might still have worn his Christmas tie every year, but only in personal remembrance. Earl Daniel would have only memories of the good times and the vision of a stricken coach through the window.

A blood drive that produced an over-abundance of supply might never have happened.

The stories told by his friends and former players would have been maudlin tales with a tearful ending.

Mike Juenger would have had no one to call at 2 a.m. to ask about deep spiritual questions in his quest for a closer relationship with God. His friend and former Unioto High teammate, who had terminal cancer, would not have had a surprise visitor to his hospital room. There wouldn't have been anyone to answer the calls from Miami Valley Hospital that said there was a burn victim – a stranger – who needed to hear someone who could speak words of comfort, words that had extra meaning because the speaker had been through everything they were enduring.

There were untold numbers of people who never would have heard the word about Jesus. He became even more deeply concerned with the spiritual well-being of old friends and acquaintances who hadn't accepted Christ.

As more people moved to Lebanon, many of the newcomers might never have known the treasure that was among them. As Daniel said, "Newer people in town might look at that marker in front of the stadium, see his name, and walk on."

But not now. James VanDeGrift is more than words on a marker. The words stand for a life of commitment, caring, and, yes, for a miracle. It's a story that needs to be told and re-told. If this had happened in ancient times, we would read it today in the Book of Vandy.

Chapter 1, Verse 1: Jim VanDeGrift pleaded with the Lord Jesus to take him home. Jesus said no.

Lives were changed forever along a two-lane road on June 5, 1997, at the city limits of Lebanon, Ohio – and not just the obvious ones.

Did the prayers of the faithful lift one of Lebanon's most cherished sons from the grip of death? Everyone involved will tell you that's what happened. They believe it. They know it.

Evil stalked Jim VanDeGrift but couldn't catch him. Death hunted him but couldn't win. Pain and anguish couldn't knock him out.

There was something bigger at stake.

When he went through the fire and came out on the other side, there was a story that needed telling, a report about faith, power and a small town's love for someone it couldn't let go. Lives needed changing. Faith needed renewing, and people on their knees waited for answers. Power had to be experienced.

Many people are better today because of that.

Was this a plan?

Ask God.

But when you do, be sure first to give thanks for the people of a little town who cared too much to give up. Then try to live an indispensable life. It's that simple. If you ever want to pay him back for the good things he has done, he will tell you that's the way.

Just walk it like you talk it and leave the rest to God.

EPILOGUE

I was a junior at Lebanon High School when Jim VanDeGrift was named head football coach. I never played for him, mostly because two years before I had been the worst player on a winless freshman team and realized I should put my athletic focus elsewhere – specifically, the press box.

Like so many others chronicled in this book, I owe a debt of thanks to Coach V. When our local Lebanon newspaper, the Western Star, needed a sports editor, he called the publisher on my behalf. I got the job at age 19 and began a career that spanned about a half-century.

I was blessed to cover national sports events like the World Series, Super Bowl, Final Four, college football championships, and so on. I spent three weeks in Athens, Greece, covering the 2004 Summer Olympics.

This book represented a way for me to say thank you, and to

highlight not only the miracle in Jim's life but also how his amazing family and a wide circle of good people in Lebanon dealt with what surely seemed like a tragedy in the making.

The VanDeGrift family is genuine, devoted, and accountable to each other, and are servant leaders. Each one of them, as I came to learn through this project, puts God first in everything and values service above self. They live to be the hands and feet of Christ.

Lebanon is my hometown. I was even born at Miami Valley Hospital, where Jim received treatment. And although my newspaper career took me to Tampa, I never forgot where I came from.

The purpose of this book was to inspire and share a n authentic message of faith in action. I hope you'll agree we succeeded because it was a group effort.

Joe Henderson, LHS Class of 1969

JoeHTampa@gmail.com

Joe Henderson

39209830R00102

Made in the USA
San Bernardino, CA
18 June 2019